TELLING 'TAILS

Leicester Animal Aid: The First 50 Years **1956 - 2006**

BY SUE ABLETT

Telling 'Tails'
Leicester Animal Aid:
The First 50 Years **1956 - 2006**
By Sue Ablett

© Leicester & Leicestershire Animal Aid
Association 2005

This edition first published in Great Britain
in 2005 by Leicester & Leicestershire
Animal Aid Association

ISBN 0-9551404-0-4

Designed and produced by
Jude Kenney
www.judemedia.co.uk

Printed in Great Britain by
AVS - Print University of Leicester
www.le.ac.uk/avs

If you would like to know more about
the work of Leicester Animal Aid, please
contact the organisation at:

**Leicester & Leicestershire
Animal Aid Association (LAA)**
The Huncote Pet Rescue Centre
Elmwood Farm
Forest Road
Huncote
Leicester
LE9 3LE

Tel (Reception): 01455 888257
Tel (Administration): 01455 888546
Email: info@leicesteranimalaid.org.uk
Web: www.leicesteranimalaid.org.uk

Registered Charity no. 242560

CONTENTS

Acknowledgements 4

Foreword 5

Author's Note 6

Dorothea Farndon: The 'Florence Nightingale of Animals' 8

Thurmaston Lane: A load of old waffle 16

The move to Huncote: Pigs might fly! 24

Joyce and Don Kelley: Dedicated or just plain daft? 30

All change: Towards the New Millenium 38

Sue Stoyell: Flatmates and Building Blocks 46

Volunteers: 'The Unsung Heroes' 58

Canine Companions: Man's Best Friend 72

Cats, rabbits and the rest: 9 lives at least 82

Reaching Out: LAA and the Community 90

The Future: Fulfilling the Dream 98

Reflections 104

Acknowledgements

Leicester Animal Aid has always been, and remains, a very special family: staff and volunteers; two and four-legged friends; old and young. So many characters, so many tales to tell. It is impossible to pay tribute to all of those people who have given so generously of their time, and often their money. Nor is it possible to include stories about all the remarkable animals, without whom there would be no story. This book features just a few, but is dedicated to all.

A great many people supplied photographs, anecdotes and recollections. We are grateful for every contribution, especially those from the following:

Sue Allcock, Margaret Allen, Vicky Arscott, Jodie Barlow, Pat Bass, Eric and Florence Bown, Janet Campion, Judith Clark, Janette Coulson, Viv Crowther, John Curzon, Pam England, Janet Evans, Claire Fish-Read, Beccy Garner, Mary Gearey, Dianne Grant, Jean Grew, Rosemary Hall, Brenda Hampson, David Harrison, Mike Hayes, Huncote Hound Club members, Joyce Kelley, Joyce Langran, Leicester Mercury (for permission to reproduce photographs), Edna Lines, Anabel McDougall, Anne Martin, Gay Martin, Josie Morris, Jackie Newman, Ken Oliver, John Rogers, Julie Rulton, Keely Short, Jan Smith, Margaret Stokes, Marion Turner, Dana Newcombe, Rita Williams, Monica Winfield.

The following contributions towards printing costs of Telling 'Tails' are acknowledged with thanks: Mrs Eileen Ablett, The Park Veterinary Group, John Rogers.

Particular thanks to Joyce Kelley, for the loan of so many photographs, and Sue Stoyell - in from the beginning of this project (those early editorial meetings were tough!). Thanks also to Jude Kenney for taking endless bundles of raw material and turning them into a commemorative history of which LAA can be very proud.

Finally, thanks to my mother for placing the first order, and my long suffering partner, John, for enduring "yet another little project".

Sue Ablett
Leicester 2005

FOREWORD
BY BILL MAYNARD

I was delighted to be asked to write the Foreword to 'Telling Tails', written to celebrate the 50th Anniversary of Leicester Animal Aid. Having lived in Leicestershire for many years, I have seen LAA grow to what it is today. It is doubtful, back in 1956, when Dorothea Farndon started taking in stray dogs and cats that she could ever have envisaged 50th anniversary celebrations, or the current scale of the animal rescue operation that she founded. Her dream has meant that literally thousands of animals have been given a second chance.

As a founder member of the cast of Heartbeat, I watched that programme grow and become a firm national favourite. All of you familiar with the roguish character of Claude Jeremiah Greengrass will know that he was rarely seen without his wonderful canine companion, Alfred. Dogs and other pets play a hugely important part in our lives and the world would be a much poorer place without them.

As actors, however, we are only too familiar with the term 'resting', which means those times when the work dries up, the money stops coming in and we have to rely on the good times to carry us through the bad. Leicester Animal Aid has seen its share of those times. Even as the 50th Anniversary celebrations are being planned there is a major crisis and possible threat of closure. That cannot be allowed to happen.

What has been achieved over the last fifty years at Leicester Animal Aid has been incredible. One woman's dream has indeed become an animal rescue and rehoming centre that is second to none, and one of which the residents of Leicestershire should be very proud. I congratulate everyone on all that has been achieved and wish every success for the next fifty years.

Bill Maynard
September 2005

AUTHOR'S NOTE
BY SUE ABLETT

As a relative newcomer to Leicester Animal Aid, the task of producing a commemorative history to mark the Association's 50th Anniversary, has been at times frustrating and challenging but, more than anything else, extremely rewarding. Delving into the past is like tracing a family tree: in this case one that is not your own, but in time begins to feel as though it could be. Getting to know Dorothea Farndon, without whom there would be no Leicester Animal Aid, through the eyes of those who knew her has been fascinating. Documenting the changes, particularly of the last few years, has felt like a rollercoaster ride, so rapid has been the progress.

It was only as recently as October 1998 that I discovered Leicester Animal Aid. It is also the day I found Fozzie – a very special Huncote Hound and a wonderful companion. Little did he realise when he chose me (at least that's his version of events) what he would be letting us in for! It is a great privilege to be part of this very special organisation, and to have had the opportunity to produce this commemorative history.

Sue Ablett
September 2005

DOROTHEA FARNDON:
THE 'FLORENCE NIGHTINGALE OF ANIMALS'

The origins of Leicester & Leicestershire Animal Aid Association, as we know it today, date back some fifty years, to 1956. The organisation owes its roots to one remarkable woman, Dorothea Farndon, known affectionately to all as "the Florence Nightingale of animals."

Dorothea Farndon, with her tame rabbit, Snowy (Leics Mercury 8 Feb 1980)

D orothea, whose family name was Hull, grew up on the Isle of Wight. Her love of animals was inherited from her mother and, even as a child, she sensed that her purpose in life would be to care for animals. When a friend wrote about a cross-bred Alsation, a stray from a German submarine, needing a home, Dorothea's mother did not hesitate and immediately took it in. Renamed Sailor Laddy, the dog became a constant childhood companion for the young Dorothea. The family subsequently moved to Leicester.

In 1932, at the age of 29, Dorothea, then working as a cashier, married Walter Hubert Farndon, a manufacturer of ladies underwear, at Blaby Register Office. Little is known of those early years, and it is not clear when the Farndons moved to the house at 86 Saffron Road, South Wigston, which was to be Dorothea's home for many years – indeed until her death in 1991. It was a beautiful house, architect-designed, large, and fortunately with a very large garden. Friends tell how, soon after moving to Saffron Road, Dorothea was disturbed by the whining of dogs in fields at the back of her house. She was horrified to discover that the method of dealing with stray dogs at that time was for them to be rounded up at a local police station and then, if not claimed within a certain period, to be taken out and shot. A local farmer had the contract to shoot the dogs. Unable to contemplate such a fate for innocent animals, Dorothea determined to go to the police station every Monday morning and buy all the doomed dogs. Apparently the first week there were 12, which she bought for 8s 6d each. Soon Dorothea was taking on every unwanted dog from the Wigston and Syston police areas, spending a lot of time and her own money. She kept some dogs, paid for temporary boarding for others, and paid all the vet's bills. And so the seeds of what was to become the Leicester and Leicestershire Animal Aid Association were sown. The Association was formally founded in 1956.

Little is known of Mr Farndon. By all accounts, Dorothea's husband did not share her love of animals. While he was still alive, strays were barred from the house, and the vet was only allowed entry through the back door. Initially, therefore, Dorothea had no option but to pay £1 a week each to board the dogs at a local kennel until homes could be found for them. Her mother's house in Cambridge Street was already being used as the office for Leicester Animal Aid and it also provided some much needed accommodation for dogs. Mr Farndon was certainly never very much in evidence. Even those who knew Mrs Farndon well, rarely met him. One volunteer of the early days recalls taking a cat to the kennels at Newton Lane, Wigston, one evening, and being completely surprised when Mr Farndon came to the door. "Not another …… cat!" was his only greeting. Some quick thinking was called for, and the volunteer managed to convince him that she was just returning a cat from a trip to the vet, not bringing yet another new one.

As the number of strays increased, it was clearly impossible for Dorothea to manage without help, and she soon began to gather around her a loyal band of animal loving friends. Funds were raised from an annual membership fee of 5s, collecting tins, coffee mornings and bring and buy sales. By June 1959 300 dogs had been rescued.

Some of those who helped out in the early days of LAA were accidental recruits to the band of volunteers. Janette Coulson (formerly Whansdell) found a stray dog that was never claimed. She ended up keeping it, and so came into contact with Mrs Farndon. Josie Morris (formerly Jones) lost her ginger cat. When it eventually returned, she was contacted by Mrs Farndon. Janette and Josie became regular volunteers, despite both having full-time jobs. "It was really difficult" recalls Janette. "We were both working full-time, we'd got animals of our own to look after, but we'd still be rushing out in the evening to collect dogs (from Wigston and Syston Police Stations), taking them to kennels, helping to rehome them. You didn't really have a choice. Mrs Farndon would ring up and just say there were dogs to be collected. So, out we would go! There was a little Austin A35 van we would use. Sometimes it would be midnight before we got home. We'd be starving and usually end up having a fry-up before we fell into bed." Janette recalls later spending two weeks holiday driving all over the place emptying collecting tins. Helping to rehome the dogs was another task. "We used to advertise the dogs" recalls Josie. "We'd always go for real tear-jerker headlines, like 'Fred wants a home – can he share your fireside?' One of the girls in my office was really good at that sort of thing. It worked every time!" Looking back on those early days they both agreed that: "You really didn't have a choice. When people knew what we were doing, they would think we were mad. But that was Mrs Farndon for you. Once you'd had any contact with her, she had you hooked!"

Janet and Martin Evans were two more volunteers from the early days, helping out with anything that needed doing, including counting out the money, and collecting and rehoming the dogs. "I remember one occasion" says Janet "we heard that two dogs whose owners had died were living in

Top: Mrs Farndon (second from left, wearing her customary hat) and some volunteers, at the LAA stall at Abbey Park Show, in the 1980s

Centre: Kelly

Bottom: Rosy

Top: Hovis
occupied the garage

Right: Henry, was Mrs Farndon's special
dog, he shared the maid's parlour with her.

Below: Lucy , who was claustrophic and
epileptic, lived in a caravan in the garden

a gypsy camp. It was completely dark but we went into that gypsy camp at dead of night to rescue those two dogs. I don't know how we dared do such a thing. Certainly no-one would do such a thing these days. But then that was Mrs Farndon for you!"

Material possessions were not something that particularly interested Dorothea Farndon. Her garden at Saffron Road was beautifully designed with fish ponds and rose gardens. For her, it meant space for chalets to house stray cats. By 1962 these were home to a total of 47 cats – a number which at the time prompted her to admit she really couldn't take any more. The cost and time involved in feeding so many animals was a major problem. Travelling between her mother's house in Cambridge Street and South Wigston, she was a regular visitor to the local fishmonger to buy up stocks of fish heads and tails – the smell on the bus home can only be imagined!

Walter Farndon died in July 1968 and, from that point on, the house in Saffron Road became home to more and more animals. It was not just the garden that served as a haven for unwanted animals. The menagerie in the house also continued to grow. There were all breeds, though Dorothea always had a strong preference for Labradors. As one visitor of the early days recalls: "The bedrooms and bathroom were all taken over by dogs. The bathroom had an amazing marble bath in the centre, but it was full of dogs. There was a beautiful grand piano in the lounge but that was full of dogs too. I remember when she came to the front door, you were greeted by what seemed like a great wall of dogs, usually with a Golden Retriever or two leading the way. The dogs were all let out into the garden in relays through the patio doors." Mrs Farndon lived in the smallest room in the house, the maid's parlour next to the kitchen. It still had all the bells round the top of the room. Even this room wasn't dog-free – it was shared with her special dog, Henry, a Golden Labrador. Other dogs, including Ben, an enormous St Bernard, lived in specially constructed compounds in the garden. A caravan in the garden was occupied by Lucy, a beautiful Red Setter, who was sadly claustrophic and epileptic. Hovis, another Labrador, occupied the garage. The cats lived in a caravan. There was dear old Billy, a lovely ginger and white cat, already an old soldier when his owner left him to Mrs Farndon. All he ever wanted as a bit of fuss and a cosy chair. Dogs, cats, rabbits – none were ever turned away. Dogs were tied at her gate, puppies left in boxes outside the gates. She took them all in. None were destroyed unless on veterinary advice. In a secluded corner, under the shade of a large tree, her beloved pets were laid to rest – many with their own individual headstones.

Dorothea Farndon had many a tale to tell about what had happened to the animals she took under her wing. Perhaps two of the most unusual to take up residence at Saffron Road were half wild cats from Bombay! They had caused a rabies scare in Wigston when they leapt from a crate from Bombay when it was being unloaded. After being at bay for three days they were found in a grain store and "sentenced" to be destroyed unless £100 could be found to pay for their stay in quarantine. Mrs Farndon not only paid the £100 but had a fine purpose-built cattery erected in her garden to house them after their release. By the time they landed on her doorstep, the mother and kitten – born in the crate on the way from Bombay – had probably used up many of their nine lives.

The house and garden at South Wigston could not accommodate all the animals that came Dorothea Farndon's way. In the early 1960s she realised a dream and acquired some land at Thurmaston Lane where she was able to put up kennels and establish her own rescue centre. Writing in the LAA Newsletter many years later, Frances Harris recalls: "This wonderful lady had a way of getting people to do things. Even if you had just staggered in from a daily stint at the kennels in Thurmaston Lane, you would be met with "Do you think you could just go to ….?"

Above: Dog cemetery

*Mrs Farndon (rarely seen without a hat) and helpers –
Thurmaston Lane*

LEICESTER MERCURY, TUESDAY, DECEMBER 22, 1987 **7**

For almost ten years those premises enabled her to take in more and more strays. In 1971 she oversaw the move to the present premises at Huncote, and continued to play an important role in overseeing developments. There was never time for holidays. She never wanted to leave her precious animals. Even in her old age she would still rise at 5am to tend "her family", and several days a week would make the bus trip to the kennels at Huncote. In 1982 she was nominated for the Leicester Mercury Roll of Honour for her remarkable achievements, something the very modest Dorothea found deeply embarassing. In December 1987, however, after over 40 years of caring for animals, Dorothea Farndon reluctantly decided to retire from leadership of the Leicester Animal Aid Committee and from her position as Treasurer. A report of her retirement in the LAA Newsletter summed up the feeling of all. "To many of us Mrs Farndon IS 'Animal Aid' and always will be." The Leicester Mercury marked her retirement with the headline "Animals' friend calls it a day". Under an editorial headed "Lifetime of caring for unwanted" a fitting tribute was paid. "People like Mrs Farndon are so very few and far between. Without them the world would be a poorer place, not only for the human beings who inhabit it, but also for the animals which so often become the victims of it. If they could speak, they could tell us so much. With Mrs Farndon, they must have known that their cries never went unheeded." Not that retirement meant a life away from her beloved animals. At that point, she still had around 60 pets at home, including a lamb called Mary and Charlie, the drake.

In the last few years of her life, it was becoming increasingly impossible for Dorothea to care for all her beloved animals. She was fortunate in having the help of a few stalwarts, particularly Dianne Grant and Ken and Jean Oliver. Dianne had first met Mrs Farndon when as a schoolgirl she performed concerts in the street near her home and donated the proceeds to Leicester Animal Aid. For around ten years, until Mrs Farndon died, Dianne was a regular visitor, spending every Saturday and Sunday, helping out and walking the dogs.

"I know it was a complete obsession" she recalls. "I never missed a weekend for about ten years, whatever the weather, but I just wanted to do something to help all the animals." With the help of Dianne, and Jean and Ken Oliver who visited in the week, Dorothea Farndon was able to keep most of the animals at home until she became ill. By the time she was admitted to hospital, shortly before her death, most of her animals had been rehomed (Diane had taken on 22 cats, and the Olivers a number of the dogs): many others had taken up residence at Huncote. Dianne then became a regular visitor at Huncote just so that the animals she had helped look after for so long would still see a friendly face.

Dorothea Farndon died on 3rd April 1991, aged 89, and is buried at Saffron Hill cemetery in Leicester, alongside her husband and parents. Those who knew her well remember her with tremendous affection, though all are equally quick to point out that she could at times be difficult, and probably fell out with most people at some point. One close friend remembers her as "a remarkable woman, completely devoted to her animals who always used to say, the more I know of people, the more I like dogs!" Another recalls that "you could never tackle Mrs Farndon. If you didn't agree with her, that was that. She could have a sharp tongue and she always liked to do things her way." There is no doubt, however, about just how much she achieved with so little. Dorothea never had children. Through the Farndon Trust, which she had set up some years earlier, her entire estate went to continuing her life-time work in caring for unwanted animals. By the time of her death, her 'one-woman' rescue operation had become a sizeable organisation. Her tireless efforts and devotion over so many years gave a chance of life to literally hundreds, if not thousands, of unwanted animals.

It was appropriate that, when Leicester Animal Aid celebrated its 40th Anniversary in 1996, the house at Huncote was renamed Farndon House. In 2002, ahead of the 50th Anniversary, the first of the newly built kennel blocks was also named in her memory. This commemorative history also serves as a fitting tribute to a remarkable woman.

THURMASTON LANE:
A LOAD OF OLD WAFFLE

It had long been a dream of Dorothea Farndon to have her own rescue centre. Eventually, in the early 1960s, that dream came true, albeit in a modest way, when a strip of land beside the road at Thurmaston Lane was found.

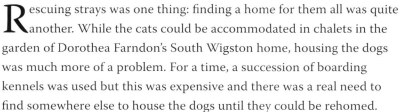

Top: *Thurmaston Lane kennels entrance*

Right: *Helper playing with the dogs at Thurmaston Lane kennels*

Below: *Butch, the deaf boxer, with Rita Williams and alone*

Rescuing strays was one thing: finding a home for them all was quite another. While the cats could be accommodated in chalets in the garden of Dorothea Farndon's South Wigston home, housing the dogs was much more of a problem. For a time, a succession of boarding kennels was used but this was expensive and there was a real need to find somewhere else to house the dogs until they could be rehomed.

The site at Thurmaston Lane was far from ideal, but it was a start, and it was hoped that eventually it would provide homes for about 30 dogs. Fences were gradually erected and wooden huts were quickly put up to house the dogs. A caravan that Mrs Farndon acquired as an office was immediately used to house a dog or two. In fact, whenever a new building went up it very quickly filled with dogs.

As the operation grew, additional help was clearly needed. Thurmaston Lane marked the early days of the volunteers. By this time, Dorothea Farndon had gathered around her a loyal band of helpers. Conditions were not good for the dogs or the volunteers – there were no toilets and nobody actually living on site, which meant that the dogs were left without attention for up to 12 hours a night. Nonetheless, stalwarts of those early days, Archibald Smith, Joyce and Don Kelley, and other volunteers worked tirelessly with the two kennel maids, Jackie (Julian) and Rita (Williams), to ensure that the dogs had the best possible care. Rita had started helping out at the kennels as a volunteer and was then offered a job as a kennel maid to help Jackie. Over thirty years later Rita still remembers many of the dogs from those early days: Butch – the deaf boxer, who would always run off because he couldn't hear, and rarely responded to hand signals; Neddy – the Labrador, a real Jekyll and Hyde, who was homed several times, but kept coming back; Ricky – the black chow, a real character. Then there was Patch, the whippet cross, who had been there so long he was completely institutionalised. He had been homed several times, but turned up at Thurmaston on his own one day and announced he was back to stay.

Initially all the kennels at Thurmaston Lane were open to the elements. It quickly became clear that if household pets were housed in open-air kennels, albeit for just a short time, they rapidly developed serious chest complaints. Some indoor kennels were needed urgently so three prefabricated huts were purchased. There was no heating in any of the kennels – the dogs would shiver in the snow and it was not unknown for dogs to die of hyperthermia.

There was water on site but it usually froze in winter. "There were icicles everywhere," recalls Jackie. "We often had to go down to the stream when the water froze." Joyce Kelley recalls that: "we had to go round knocking on the doors of the nearby industrial units to ask the security guards for water, or I would persuade Don to load water into the panniers of the scooter and take it to Thurmaston Lane just to make sure the dogs always had fresh drinking water."

Feeding the dogs was always a challenge. Waffle (a kind of frozen offal) was the staple diet. Often it was still frozen and had to be taken home, again in the panniers of the Kelley scooter, to be put in front of the fire to thaw, before being taken back again later in the day. The smell in the house as it thawed out was not for the faint-hearted! The neighbouring factory would provide leftovers from the canteen to help feed the dogs. As a child, Mary Gearey's father worked in a factory opposite the kennels. She and her sister would regularly pack up food parcels for the dogs. With big gates at the site, there was no option but to throw the parcels over the gate. At Christmas there were extra special food parcels.

Some of the volunteers went to remarkable lengths to care for the dogs. Two elderly ladies, Mrs Bell and Mrs Hart, would travel to Thurmaston Lane by bus every day, often bringing rice puddings to feed the puppies. At that time dogs often came in with distemper – a dreadful disease for which, in those days, there was no vaccination. Mrs Bell, in particular, was devoted to nursing the sick dogs. She would bring bread poultices with her on the bus and, if necessary, sit up all night in an old wooden hut with a sick dog. Lack of funds meant it was not always possible to call in the vet when a dog was sick, so the old remedies were used in those early days. Cold tea was used for bathing sore eyes. Chest infections were treated by inhaling Friar's Balsam in hot water. For complications of distemper a kaolin poultice on the chest was held in place with a flannel jacket, laced up round the back.

Helpers with the dogs and tea at the Thurmaston Lane kennels

With no staff living on site, it was usual at Thurmaston Lane to unlock the gates and greet the dogs. Frances Harris, writing in the LAA Newsletter, recalled that one morning was different. "I was met by a brindle lurcher who welcomed me like a long lost friend. Thinking he had got in and couldn't get out, I let him out to go home. On turning round he was behind me. After a couple of repeats of this performance, I watched him. He went out of the gate, down the field alongside and leapt the 6-8 ft

chain link fence. He decided he was staying – but not for nothing! Bryn guarded those kennels with his life, but could not be caged – he had to be free. One evening I had to go there to leave some stuff: there were no lights so I had to use the van headlights to see. The next moment Bryn was at the gate and believe me, if I hadn't known him, I wouldn't have gone near the place. Fortunately, he soon recognised me but I realised just how much he was giving back for his home and his food. We learned he had come to us from some travellers and, as is often the case, two little friends soon followed. Smokie a grey lurcher was in a sorry state. We could see the bones in her tail. The white one was even worse. One Sunday afternoon saw the young helpers bathing these two, and the difference was amazing. After weeks of good feeding and care, they looked like different dogs. They would all meet us at the gate, grinning the way this breed does. Does a dog say thank you? These certainly did!"

Finances were always tight in those days. On many occasions when the food stocks were running low, the loyal volunteers would take to the streets for door to door collections. This often meant going up and down garden paths, sometimes at 10 o'clock at night, trying to bring in enough money to feed the dogs for the next week. Sometimes they would be given bones direct from the abattoir: these were boiled up in an old copper.

"We used to have wonderful Christmas bazaars" recalls one of the early volunteers, Joyce Langran. "They were held at St John's Church Rooms in Clarendon Park Road. We would all take things to sell. There were always stalls selling home-made goodies and groceries, pickles and jams. Mrs Farndon used to come along with Mr Smith – one of the founders of LAA - and count the takings in the rear room. Then there was always a speech of thanks to the helpers from Mr Smith." Josie Morris ran a jewellery stall at the Christmas bazaar. "I would collect beads, wash them and rethread them. The dealers always used to come first thing. You could always tell them by their grubby hands. We always doubled the price when we thought it was a dealer!" At one point Mr Smith's wife, Irene, ran a stall on Leicester Market, and there was also a little shop in Cavendish Road, a side street off Aylestone Road.

In no time at all the kennels at Thurmaston Lane were stretched to the absolute limit. Sometimes dogs were brought in by their owners who threatened to have them destroyed if they weren't accepted. Sometimes they were simply left, tied to the gate. More often than not, the dogs were found roaming the streets, often having been turned

Above: Bryn

Left: Mr Smith

out by a callous owner. In 1967, with the kennels bursting at the seams with 60 dogs in residence, and more coming in all the time, Mr Archibald Smith, then chairman of LAA, launched an urgent appeal for good homes for the dogs and for much needed financial assistance. At that point the running costs amounted to £30 a week and the burden of raising the running costs, plus the costs of acquiring kennel accommodation, at times threatened to become too much. Talk of closure was not uncommon. Somehow, the situation was salvaged again and again. Good local publicity would result in a number of dogs being homed successfully, or an increase in donations, but then they would soon face the same crisis again and again.

Above: Mr Smith and Lassie

Brenda Hampson remembers visiting Thurmaston Lane in the late 60's. "We were looking for a dog. The place was really tatty, but Mrs Farndon was wonderful and it was amazing what she was doing there. We settled for a dog, called Happy. He was a bearded collie cross, so scruffy and so forlorn. We just thought – well if we don't take him, no-one else will. They warned us that he'd been homed twice and brought back because he chewed all the furniture. We certainly wondered what we were taking on. But he was only about two and we felt he needed a chance. We took him home and he never put a foot wrong. He was wonderful, such a lovely nature. We changed his name to Laddie. He idolised my husband, and not long after my husband died, Laddie died too. We had him for about ten years – he was just the most wonderful dog."

Memories of Dorothea Farndon vary. She certainly had a reputation for being difficult some times. As one volunteer of those early days recalled "there was more than one occasion when we used to hide in the kennels just to keep out of her way!"

After struggling on with desperately cramped accommodation, they eventually managed to rebuild the premises at Thurmaston Lane. In May 1968 the "new spacious kennels" were officially opened by the Rev John Garratt, rector of All Saints, Narborough. At that time there were sixty dogs in residence and all labour, apart from the two part-time kennel maids, was provided by volunteers.

Conditions at Thurmaston Lane were never ideal. 1970, however, saw the start of a the biggest crisis the Association had ever faced when a letter was received, informing them that most of the land occupied by

the kennels in Thurmaston Lane was needed for redevelopment, and they had just one week's notice to quit. Although there had been talk of redevelopment for some time, no-one anticipated being given so little time to make alternative arrangements. The land was in two halves – a 50ft wide strip alongside the road owned by the Corporation, the rest by Bernard Wheatcroft Ltd, a firm of builders. The problem was that most of the bigger kennels were sited on the Wheatcroft half and even if there had been room on the Corporation strip a water main prevented kennels from being put up there. The lives of the 100 – 115 dogs were at real risk. The majority of dogs faced being put down if new homes couldn't be found for them, or if alternative premises couldn't be found. Mr Smith, ill in bed with flu at the time, launched a passionate appeal for help, hoping that someone could offer some land, or that people would give the dogs a home – even if only temporary. After appealing to the County Council, to whom the rent had always been paid, the Association was allowed to keep a narrow strip of land on the edge of the original site. At the same time there was a promise of alternative accommodation, though none actually materialised. Whenever a new site was found, planning permission was always refused for one reason or another. With an appeal in the local paper, Mrs Huckbody, spokesperson for the Association, explained that things were so desperate they would rent or buy any suitable piece of land for which they could get planning permission. By October of that same year the situation was clearly becoming impossible, and it was not clear how much longer they could carry on.

Pressure to find alternative kennel accommodation was becoming critical. As one of the volunteers in the early days recalls: "Building work at Thurmaston Lane meant we had to reduce drastically the number of kennels. Then the owner was bulldozing all the fences, so the dogs kept escaping. It was a complete nightmare! The local paper was full of it – I can still see the headlines even now!" In a final desperate attempt to solve the accommodation problem, a decision was taken to advertise for a piece of land where they could build kennels for over 100 dogs. Although efforts were being made to reduce the number of dogs, there were still around 70 to 80 on a piece of land really only big enough for half that number: two or three dogs were regularly sharing a kennel.

Scouring the neighbourhood for alternative sites was a time-consuming process but, once again, LAA's loyal supporters saved the day. It just so happened that Joyce Langran, a committed volunteer, worked for local architect, Mr John Wilmot. Unwittingly, he found himself being roped in to help. Together they trudged around Leicestershire, in thick snow, looking at possible sites. "There were only the two of us, so the office was often left empty," recalls Joyce, "but we were under such pressure to find somewhere, and fast, that we really had no choice."

A number of alternative sites were considered, but for one reason or another, none came to fruition. Eventually, in desperation, a plea for help was made to County Hall. It was suggested that the area around Huncote might be worth exploring as a number of pig farmers were likely to be giving up their farms. After much banging on farmers' doors, a former pig farm at Huncote (the present premises) was found. The farmer was about to retire, and planned to move away from the area, so was willing to sell the farm lock, stock and barrel.

So, at the eleventh hour, the prayers were answered and the search was over. All that remained was to find the money to buy the Huncote farm, obtain the necessary planning permission, and organise the move! A new chapter in the story of Leicester Animal Aid was about to unfold.

NEW HOME FOR LOST DOGS

FOR several years the Leicester Animal Aid Association has been caring for lost and ill-treated dogs—normally at the rate of about 500 a year. After using cramped accommodation, they have now rebuilt the premises at their Thurmaston Lane centre.

And their new spacious kennels were officially opened yesterday—marking great progress by the association since it was founded by Mrs. Dorothea Farndon, 65, Cambridge Road, about eight years ago.

At the moment there are 60 dogs in the association's kennels. All labour, apart from two part-time kennel maids, is entirely voluntary.

Opening the new kennels, the Rev. John Garratt, rector of All Saints, Narborough, said that man's use of animals was not all it should be, and people had a duty to protect animals from cruelty and exploitation.

THE MOVE TO HUNCOTE:

PIGS MIGHT FLY!

For Leicester Animal Aid, the new four-acre site
at Huncote offered tremendous opportunities,
though a former pig farm did not exactly come
ready for instant occupancy as a kennels.

14 LEICESTER MERCURY, WEDNESDAY, DECEMBER 30, 197

FUND TO BE LAUNCHED

Kennels plan gets council go-ahead

BLABY RURAL COUNCIL have approved planning permission for new kennels run by the Leicester Animal Aid Association on a four-acre site at Huncote.

The approval was given at a meeting yesterday. It will mean the construction in the near future of 100-150 kennels, all built to the specifications of the Animal Aid Association.

The news of the council's decision will mark the launching of a money-raising campaign by the association to pay for the kennels.

The chairman of the Leices-

as much as 12 hours or more without attention."

Mr. Smith said that no campaign to raise funds had been launched before planning permission had been approved.

He said: "We have been wait-

...UND TO BE LAUNCHED

...ennels plan ...ets council go-ahead

BLABY RURAL COUNCIL have approved planni
...ission for new kennels run by the Leicester Ani
...sociation on a four-acre site at Huncote.
...approval was given at a meeting yeste...
...he construction in the near future ...
...ilt to the specifications of th...

(Partially visible planning application form)

County Council Ref. No.

...Council No. .

...ceived by ...rict Council

COUNTY OF LEICESTER
Town and Country Planning Acts
APPLICATION FOR PERMISSION TO DEVELOP LAND
(Three copies of this application with plans and one copy of either
Certificate "A","B","C" or "D" are required)

{ Borough
{ Urban District Cou...
{ Rural District

To the ....BLABY...

If signed by an Agent

Name and Address of Applicant
(IN BLOCK LETTERS)

Surname (state whether Mr., Mrs. or Miss)
....ANIMAL AID ASSOCIATION

Other Names......

Postal Address c/o J W WILMOT
53, HINCKLEY RD., LEICESTER

Telephone No... 26848

Name of Agent: JOHN W.WILM...
Profession........ARCHITECT...
Address of Agent 53, HINCKL...
....LEICES...
Telephone No....... 26848

PART I—GENERAL
(In this part the word "land" includes any buildings thereon.)

(1) Address or location of the land to be developed,
in sufficient detail to enable it to be readily
identified. (See notes on Site Plans.)

(1) ....ELMWOO...
......FOREST ...
......HU...

...riefly the proposed development,
... for which the land and/or

(2) ....

Above: Appeal for funds is launched

Below: Settling the dogs in: day one

Finding the site at Huncote was a start. There was then, of course, the critical problem of how to pay for it. The sale price of £7,500, plus a further £2,500 for alterations, was way beyond the budget. The money had to be borrowed, something of a gamble at the time. The help of two benefactors of those early days, Mrs Carver and Miss Garvey, was critical in enabling LAA to go ahead and not only commit to the site, but also embark on the necessary alterations.

Since there were already buildings on the site, the planning regulations were fairly straightforward: the only requirement was an application for change of use. In December 1970, Blaby Rural Council approved planning permission for the new kennels – a move which could eventually mean the construction of 100-150 kennels on the site.

The Huncote site was filthy, full of dirt and debris, and required a huge clean up operation before many dogs could be housed. Pigs had been slaughtered at the farm, so a lot of carcasses had to be cleared before the premises could be occupied. In fact, for many years afterwards pig carcasses were still being dug up. A big advantage with the site was that it included a house, albeit in a pretty bad state. It did mean, however, that for the first time it would be possible to have somebody living permanently on site.

Given the crisis at Thurmaston Lane, there was a need to move quickly to organise accommodation for the dogs. Anything that could be brought from Thurmaston Lane was brought. The caravan and some of the dog kennels were moved. A scrap metal merchant moved 400 concrete slabs from Thurmaston Lane to Huncote, free of charge. Initially, one pig-sty was used to house dogs, another provided useful storage space. Thanks yet again to the intervention of local architect, Mr Wilmot, negotiations with Leicester City Council proved a vital source of kennel accommodation in the form of post-war prefabs. A number of these were acquired, moved to the site, and hastily partitioned to form kennel accommodation.

Everything was done in a hurry, but there was a desperate need to move the dogs from Thurmaston Lane. Dorothea Farndon took personal responsibility for supervising the move to Huncote. "The move itself was a nightmare" recalls volunteer Joyce Langran, "but everyone helped. We all took one or two dogs. Some of them were not easy to handle, but somehow we made it and they were all safely installed in their new home."

The farm was all that Dorothea Farndon and her helpers could have hoped for. The intention was to modernise the whole farm eventually, in order to provide room for more than 100 dogs in ideal surroundings, more than they had ever been able to accept in the past. Money was a continual problem, and initially the situation was desperate. It hadn't been possible to launch a campaign to raise funds until planning permission had been granted. Once that was in hand, Dorothea Farndon launched an urgent appeal for funds. Permission was granted to carry out a house-to-house collection in the city and county, but helpers were desperately needed. So an appeal for more volunteers was also launched.

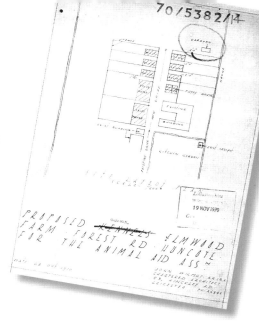

Less than six months after the move, on 20th June 1971, the Association held its first Open Day at the new premises. The Leicester Mercury report of the event gives an indication of what a successful start it was to be. "Cars were parked alongside Forest Road for almost the entire mile and a quarter from the kennel to Huncote Village, and by supporting a number of stalls in the grounds visitors helped raise £225 towards the costs of establishing the association in its new premises." People apparently flocked to the kennels in their hundreds. One of the dogs that attracted considerable attention was a one year old Alsation cross bitch, found tied to a fence at Thurnby, and in such a dreadful state that the dog, subsequently named Penny, could barely stand. Once taken in to LAA, she recovered well, and gave birth to puppies just before Open Day.

Above: Site plan

Below: Grey Judy with Joyce Kelley and Rita Williams with puppies

The first residents at Huncote were a motley crew: Bobby, totally blinded when slashed with chains by his owner and abandoned by another 'master' who took pity on him; Johnny, a laughing greyhound taken to Huncote by Derby police, and Jenny – a four month old bitch thrown from a moving car. Grey Judy (right) was to become one of the longest survivors of the dogs who moved from Thurmaston Lane. She eventually died in 1984, aged 14, having spent the greater part of her life at Huncote.

Those early years at Huncote saw a succession of kennel managers, and helpers. Firstly, there was local couple, Mr and Mrs Pitcher. Mr Pitcher used to work at the Stadium - the Leicester home of greyhound racing - and remained a great greyhound fan. Eventually they both moved into the house. They were helped by kennel maid, Rita Williams, and Jackie Julian, who had both worked previously at Thurmaston Lane. The

Above: Iris Becker

Below: Miss Turner presents the new ambulance to Mr Smith. Arnold Becker with Sadie

Pitchers were followed by Arnold and Iris Becker, who moved up from London, bringing seven dogs of their own with them. When Arnold subsequently left to go back to London, Iris continued to run the Centre, with the help of kennel maids and volunteers, until her death in 1977.

Life at Huncote in those very early days was certainly far from easy. For a time, with no manager living in, Rita found herself living in an old caravan on site. When Iris was left to run the kennels on her own, Jackie moved into the house. "We worked from daylight to dusk, " recalls Jackie. "We had one day a week off if we were lucky. There was no heat in the house, just an old Valor heater, and it was full of mice. If you left a box of chocolates lying around, it would be empty when you next went to it! We ate the same thing every day – Fray Bentos steak and kidney pie out of a tin. We were just too tired to do anything else. Often we never actually went to bed. We would settle down in a chair by the heater, with the dogs all round us, and wake up in the morning without having moved. And the smell on our clothes, particularly from the food we had to cook up was dreadful. It all came from the abattoir – ox tongues and cows udders. You name it, it would all go into the big old copper, and we then had to mix it up in big old baths. The kitchen got so hot in summer. I can still picture the fly papers hanging from the ceiling. I used to go home to my mother's once a week. It was quite a walk down to Huncote to get the bus, always carrying bags of washing. As I walked in the house my brother would always say he could smell the dirty washing coming down the street!"

Another legacy of Thurmaston Lane days was the old general purpose van. It had given wonderfully devoted service collecting dogs from all over the place, but was never going to pass another M.O.T. test. As happened so many times over the years, the loyal band of supporters came to the rescue. Margaret Allen of Birstall had acquired an Alsation, called Tanya, from LAA, and was keen to help in whatever way was needed. So when Mrs Farndon mentioned to her the need for a new vehicle, the ambulance fund was born. Margaret at that time was manager of a local building society branch office, and Tanya was a regular in the office. Tanya quickly acquired a lot of friends, and word spread about LAA. Customers regularly contributed items of food. Once the ambulance fund was launched, there was great support locally for all the fund-raising efforts, mainly coffee mornings and treasure hunts by bicycle into the surrounding countryside.

The cost of the new ambulance was about £1,100. Progress was slow but a donation of £500 from LAA benefactor, Miss F.G. Turner, also of Birstall, meant that the ambulance could be purchased. Margaret was to become a regular visitor to Miss Turner, then an old lady, but still Director of the family firm of W & E Turner, Shoe Manufacturers. "Miss Turner was a friend of Mrs Farndon", recalls Margaret. "They were very much alike in many ways, very strong-minded, and Miss Turner was a real animal lover. She would always say, whenever you're trying to do anything to raise money, do come and see me." So it was only appropriate that when the first new ambulance was purchased, in 1973, it was Miss Turner who handed it over to the Chairman of LAA, Mr Archibald Smith, and Arnold Becker, then Manager. The first passenger in the new ambulance, was Sadie, a two-year old, three-legged bitch, who needed treatment after giving birth to four pups only two days after she was brought in as a stray.

Above: Beauty, in his cart

Below: Mrs Turner laying the foundations and the formal opening of the new hospital

Other dogs of those early days remembered with affection by Rita and Jackie were Greyhounds, Mike and Lady; Zak, a large Alsation and Gay; Rupert, a Terrier X who never wanted to get up in the morning; Jason, a Beagle – lovely looking but very unpredictable; Marcus, a Dalmation, with odd eyes; and Trish, a Saluki, who had to have her front leg amputated. Beauty, always a happy dog, had been in a car accident, and dragged his back legs. Life for Beauty was transformed when volunteer, Ken Oliver, made him a little cart to take his weight.

Miss Turner proved to be a very generous benefactor of the early days, funding the building of the first Hospital block. In 1974, under the ever watchful eye of Dorothea Farndon, and in the presence of other loyal supporters, she laid the Foundation Stone. This was followed by a grand opening, with blessing. Once in use, the Hospital was occupied by the very old dogs, who were able to potter around together, as well as the very young.

It is doubtful that anyone envisaged that the original pig sties would be in use for very long, but it was 1995, over 20 years after the move to Huncote, when Enderby Young Farmers stepped in to lend a hand, that the last of the original pig sties was demolished. A real end of an era!

JOYCE AND DON KELLEY:
DEDICATED OR JUST PLAIN DAFT?

It was 1969 and Joyce Kelley could never have
predicted just how much a good deed for a little
brown collie dog was going to change for ever her
life, or that of husband, Don.

Above: Joyce Kelley with Lisa

Below: Cleaning the kennels

On her way to work one morning, Joyce saw a little brown collie – a bitch obviously in season – surrounded by all the dogs in the neighbourhood. She had to get to work and couldn't stop. On the way home the dog was still there. Joyce managed to catch her, found out where she lived, and tried to return her to her owners. They weren't interested, even when Joyce enlisted the help of two bobbies on the beat. Although the Kelley household already had its fair share of dogs and cats, as well as Joyce's mother living with them, Joyce took the dog home with her. "How many more?" was her mother's immediate response. The dog couldn't stay with them long term and Joyce spent a frantic evening, poring through the phone book trying to find details of any animal rescue centre. Eventually she spotted Leicester Animal Aid Association at Cambridge Street. Dorothea Farndon answered the phone and said of course they would take the dog. At eleven o'clock that evening, two volunteers came to collect her. For Joyce, any organisation that would turn out at that time of night to help a dog in distress, had to be something special. For the little collie dog, there was a very happy ending. She was taken into kennels, where she proceeded to produce a litter of puppies, and was then found a home with one of the kennel maids. For Joyce this was the start of a long association with Dorothea Farndon and Leicester Animal Aid, as she found herself immediately enlisted as one of the volunteers at Thurmaston Lane.

Despite having full-time jobs, Joyce and husband, Don, became regular weekend helpers, firstly at Thurmaston Lane and then at Huncote. By 1977 they were living in Croft. They would usually stop off at Huncote early in the morning on their way to work. One particular morning in 1977, Iris Becker, who had been trying to run the kennels single-handed after the departure of her husband, was due to go into hospital, and Rita, the kennel maid, who also lived in the house, was still in bed. There were dogs everywhere – six poodles in the front room, Iris's seven dogs in her room, and about 120 outside in the kennels. Joyce's response was to tell Don to go to work that day, and to say she wouldn't be in that day as her mother was ill. In fact, she never did go back to work!

"It was complete chaos that morning" recalls Joyce. "It was nine o'clock before I'd finished cleaning up the house – well, with all those dogs you can imagine the state it was in. And then we had to start on the kennels." Joyce's action in giving up a well paid job was remarkable. Don was amazingly understanding about a move which cost Joyce her entire pension. "Well he knew what I was like" said Joyce. Her mother, who was living with them in Croft, was less understanding. "In fact she went berserk. Whenever anyone wanted to know where I was, all mother would say is "She's gone to the dogs - again!" And so began a way of life for Joyce that would mean seven day weeks, and no holidays for the next seventeen years!

Iris Becker died in 1977. A short time afterwards Joyce was formally appointed Manager, for which she was paid the princely sum of £80 a month. "It was much less than I had been paid" said Joyce "and there was no holiday pay, no pension. You couldn't get away with it these days! We used to get paid in coppers from the collecting tins. You can imagine what it was like going to the Co-op to do the week's shopping, carrying this bag full of coins." For a while, Don continued to work full-time, helping out at the kennels every weekend. In 1982, probably working on the principle that in order to see something of Joyce, he had better join her, he gave up his job and was appointed Assistant Manager.

"Life certainly wasn't easy in those days" recalls Joyce. "For a start all the dogs used to spend the days in wire pens. That meant we had to move them all out in the morning, and move them all back in the evening. We had so many dogs. Mrs Farndon couldn't ever say no, so sometimes we had two or three in one run. In the early days the sleeping quarters were tiny confined areas in cold outhouses. The wire pens had no shelter and the dogs would stand outside all day, in all weathers, and at all times of the year. A cheese and wine party held at Janet Campian's house meant they could buy outside kennels for each pen where the dogs could shelter from the sun or rain, or just find a bit of peace and quiet. It made such a difference for the dogs. It was amazing though how many people thought the dogs lived in those little huts. They were really surprised when they knew we had to take the dogs in every night.

"The kennels were old. Cleaning out the dogs was hard work. The floors were pitted. There were wooden pens, which were a health hazard and certainly wouldn't be acceptable by today's standards. There were no drains in some of the blocks so they were really difficult to wash down. Initially the dogs slept on wooden pallets. Volunteer, Ken Oliver, took on the task of using the wood from the pallets to make proper wooden beds. They were filled with straw which was changed every Saturday – a huge improvement for the dogs.

Above: Aerial view of Huncote and Don with Rex

Below: Nip, and Joyce with the dogs

Above: Garden

Below: Lady the Greyhound and a volunteer preparing bowls

"Feeding all the dogs was like a military exercise. There was just one kitchen to serve all the blocks. Fresh meat from the slaughter house had to all be cut up before being cooked up every day in a huge gas boiler. Everything was thrown in – all kinds of vegetables, and Bovril. The dogs loved it. And then Don would go round to collect up all the bowls and take them all a bit of 'pudding'. For Christmas Dinner we went to more trouble. Mr Smith always used to put an article in the Leicester Mercury appealing for food to help with the dogs Christmas dinner."

These were difficult times in every respect. Money was always tight. Joyce knew there was never any point asking for anything. The Committee wasn't prepared to spend money it couldn't afford. Mrs Farndon took a different line, always prepared to spend what she hadn't got – a source of much 'debate' in Committee meetings. Meetings would go on into the evening, decisions be made. Then Joyce's phone would ring. She always knew it would be Mrs Farndon. "Forget what's just been decided" she would say, "I'm the boss." Mrs Farndon's same direct approach also had an impact on the kennel staff, with more than one kennel maid packing her bags and walking out after an 'encounter' with Mrs F.

Without the support of loyal volunteers and Committee members, life would have been exceptionally difficult. Mrs Carver and Miss Garvey continued to provide generous support in a variety of ways. Committee meetings were always held at Mrs Carver's house, and it was her gardener who ensured that the gardens and cemetery were always immaculate. Iris and George Kirk helped with the shop, rebuilt and enlarged in 1984, manned stalls to raise funds, and spread the word as they travelled round in their motor caravan. Jean and Ken Oliver helped out in so many ways over many years. Mr Smith, one of the original helpers, was one of the earliest dog walkers. "He was a lovely man" recalls Joyce, "though he could be a bit forgetful. The number of times he would let the greyhounds out for a last run, and go home and forget them. The phone would ring, and I always knew what he was going to say. By then, we had usually found them and put them away."

In 1978, despite an objection by Huncote Parish Council concerned about the Association breaking away from its original aim, Blaby District Council Planning Committee granted permission to erect 18 new boarding kennels at Huncote. The expansion would mean some welcome extra income over the busy summer months. Provision of boarding kennels was welcomed by many owners, who were reluctant to go away on holiday

unless they knew Don would be looking after their dogs. The kennels were to be built thanks to a donation by association vice-chairman, Mr John Maher, a builder from Tipperary, who had supported the Group since it started, both with building work and fund raising.

Money was always tight, though never quite as bad as Thurmaston Lane days when they never seemed to know where the next meal was coming from. The Open Days were better, there were bigger raffles, and one or two legacies began to come in.

In 1981 LAA faced yet another crisis as the ambulance, bought in 1973, reached the end of its life. That little white van, bought from donations, had notched up 60,000 miles, collecting unwanted or abandoned dogs, taking sick and injured dogs for veterinary treatment, re-uniting owners with their lost dogs and taking rescued dogs to good and caring homes. Many dogs owed their lives to the mercy missions. And so an appeal was launched for the £3,000 needed to buy a new vehicle. Eventually a replacement was bought with Ricky, the whippet, found down a well, the first dog to use the new ambulance.

In 1982, completely out of the blue a legacy of £50,000 meant that the first new kennel block could be built. The donor was a Mrs Molly Carabine, who as a young girl had enjoyed visiting the South Wigston home of Dorothea Farndon to admire her large collection of stray cats and dogs. She went on to become a successful businesswoman, and owner of a local hotel. Prior to her death she had been a keen supporter of Leicester Animal Aid, regularly bringing stocks of white overalls for the staff and volunteers to wear. Molly Carabine's legacy was remembered in June 1982, when her business partner, Mr G.J. Porter, opened a new block of purpose built kennels – just one of the improvements made possible by the legacy. Others included a facelift for most of the existing kennels and modernising the kitchen where meals for a hundred dogs were prepared daily.

Presentation of the new ambulance, with Ricky, the whippet who was the first dog to use it.

These were not easy times. The task of taking the dogs out into their runs every morning and bringing them back in at night was a huge task for staff, though many of the dogs would almost find their own way into their night quarters. Initially the only block with any heating was the Hospital. Water would freeze in the others, and it was not unknown for dogs to develop hyperthermia.

HERE LIES. RUSTY 1963-1978 FAITHFUL FRIEND RIP BEAUTIFUL

Above: Dog Cemetery

Left: Rusty's memorial stone

Below: Jess and Jess' puppies

It was only in the mid 1980s that money was raised to buy insulation blocks that volunteer, Ken Oliver, built inside the thin outer skin of the building, to keep the dogs warmer. Electric heaters were purchased and installed in each block. The pens were all repainted. The dog walking scheme got off the ground in 1986 and subsequently a more formal system of home checking began.

Although there was a policy of homing dogs, for many LAA dogs, the kennels were to provide a lasting home – in many cases the best they had ever had - and their final resting place – in the area set aside as the Dog Cemetery. "It was amazing" recalls Joyce, "Don was always walking round the site carrying sacks of this and that. But whenever a dog had died and he was carrying it to the cemetery to be buried, the whole kennels would fall silent. It was as if they all knew. Don used to dig all the graves. I can still see him now, when Freebie, the huge Pyrennean Mountain Dog died. You could hardly see him, the hole was so big." Each dog that died was recorded on the Memorial Board and, in the case of Rusty, one of Mr Smith's favourite greyhounds, a memorial stone was erected.

Over the years a large number of waifs and strays passed through the kennels and benefited from the loving care of Joyce and Don. They all had tales to tell, and all were special in their own way. But one in particular captured their hearts. It was a Sunday afternoon, early in January 1983, when a man was out walking his dog, Kerry – an Irish setter, across the fields in Leicester Forest East. Kerry, usually obedient and quick to return when called, would not leave an old car wreck at the side of the field. Puzzled, the man went to see what was bothering his dog. To his amazement, he saw that she had found a cardboard box containing four puppies. Three unfortunately were dead, and the fourth barely clinging to life. He took it straight to the kennels at Huncote. She was a pathetic scrap of life, very very weak, and her chances of survival were not good. With much love and care, however, the black and white rough terrier, not only pulled through but made a full recovery. By this time, Lucky Lucy, as she had been called, was very much part of the Kelley household, and became a much loved part of the family for the next sixteen years. Over that time she went to the kennels every day, and made friends with many hundreds of dogs. She took everything in her stride and whatever sick or elderly dog was brought home overnight, Lucy would just sit quietly with them all night. By the time Lucy died in December 1998 she had given 16 years of untold love and happiness with her cute and loveable ways.

Over the years there were a great many dogs that passed through the gates: the dogs brought in as strays, those handed in by owners who could no longer afford them, the puppies who had ceased to be a novelty, the casualties of divorce, or ill health or death of their owners. There were the three adorable puppies left in a bucket outside the front gate overnight. Jess, a mongrel bitch, was put out on the streets by her owners when she was found to be having pups. By the time she was taken into LAA, Jess was starving with barely sufficient strength to stand. She went on to produce 12 healthy pups. Roly, a Cardigan Corgi, terrorised all who came near him. With a policy of never putting a dog to sleep except on veterinary advice, many dogs spent much of their lives at Huncote.

Another real favourite from 'the Kelley era' was Dogsey, a Bull Terrier cross Labrador, who was handed in originally by his owners as an unwanted pet. His death in 1987 was marked in the local paper by the headline 'Dogsey makes his last escape ...'. Dogsey, who had spent 14 of his 15 and a half years at Huncote, was a favourite of staff, volunteers and visitors alike. "He was a real rogue" recalls Joyce " a lovable mischief-maker and escapologist. He was one of our oldest residents and enjoyed some special privileges, such as a glass fronted kennel near the entrance. He earned his tearaway reputation because he pulled so much when he was walked and he always made a real fuss at lights-out. He was a real Houdini. Two seconds and he would be out, even from a covered run, with wire on the top. He did go to a home once but he didn't last very long. On open days, people would bring him chicken sandwiches and he used to try and help out on the stalls. He would go through the rummage and collect toys to take back to his kennel. And if ever you were making a cup of tea, he always had to have a dish. He really was such a character."

'Walkies are over for Centre's leading lights' was the headline in the local paper to mark the retirement of Joyce and Don, in October 1993. For the first time in seventeen years there was a prospect of a day off, or even a holiday. They never could agree on whether they had been "truly dedicated" as many claimed or "just plain daft" as they preferred to describe what was a truly remarkable period in their lives, and of LAA.

Top: Don with Roly

Centre: Roly

Bottom: Dogsey

Left: Joyce and Don at their retirement

ALL CHANGE:
TOWARDS THE NEW MILLENIUM

Around 1990 the Committee had to consider the future of the kennels. The dilemma was whether to remain at Huncote and rebuild both above and below ground, or relocate.

rior to 1980 the kennel blocks were cold and draughty. There was no heating at all, rain or snow beat in at some points, water bowls froze over in extreme temperatures and hyperthermia was a real problem. It was a sad sight to see the dogs, especially the old ones, on cold winter mornings. The pens were very small, and often housed two or more dogs. There were no runs attached, so each day the dogs had to be taken to outside pens where they panted with the heat in summer and shivered in cold winter winds, rain and snow. Something needed to be done to make the dogs more comfortable.

Above: A Block and Don Crowther, Dana Newcombe and wife Viv

During the 1980s, while Joyce and Don Kelley, were in charge of LAA, a number of steps were taken to improve the welfare of the dogs. The dog walking scheme was started; outside kennels were bought, one for each pen, to provide shelter for the dogs during the day; money was raised to buy insulated bricks to keep the dogs warmer; electric heaters were purchased for each block and, lastly, a more formal system of home checking was introduced. A start had been made but much more was needed.

Around 1990 it was becoming increasingly obvious that kennel and house repairs were urgently needed, and drainage and sewage pipes would need renewing. The Committee had to consider the future of the kennels. The dilemma was whether to remain at Huncote and rebuild both above and below ground, or relocate. Much thought was given to this and it was eventually decided to stay put, and rebuild entirely, beginning with the Boarding Block. The adjacent field, purchased by the Committee in the 1990's brought the area up to a 4 and a half acre site, allowing more scope for development. For the Committee, the whole concept represented an enormous challenge, one which required both vision and commitment.

Below: The old boarding block

At this time Animal Aid had a very forward looking Committee, under the leadership of Sue Allcock (Chair) and Pat Bass (Secretary), and all were totally dedicated to animal welfare, as were the Trustees, Don Crowther and Eric Bown. They were prepared to plan and work towards a massive development within the decade preceding the Millenium, and were determined that animals coming into the care of LAA in future would have nothing but the best. The Committee's vision was to change the antiquated, dilapidated kennel situation into a new, vibrant, modern sanctuary for dogs and cats, the welfare of the animals being given the highest priority.

The site needed to be rebuilt from scratch so that all animals would be housed in warm, light, airy pens with access to outside covered runs. They deserved no less, the aim being that, as far as possible, the animals in the care of LAA would have the same level of care enjoyed by pets in loving homes. They would be given good nutrition, the best veterinary care, equal to that given to well-loved animals at home and each animal would be treated with respect, as an individual, names on pens helping staff, volunteers and visitors to call the animals by name thereby ensuring plenty of interaction and TLC. The vision was that LAA would be one of the foremost Shelters in the country with regard to the high standard of care given to the animals seeking refuge and help, the Shelter being a secure and happy environment for them while they awaited new homes.

Whilst the Committee could draw up policies, they realised that to achieve the vision, professional help would be needed with rebuilding work on the site. The links between Leicester Animal Aid and Wood Green Animal Shelters date from this period. WGAS was a first-class, modern homing centre for all kinds of animals, with an innovative approach to kennelling dogs, and superb housing for cats. They also ran training courses for kennel staff and managers. An approach was made to Wood Green to see whether they would consider acting as Consultants to LAA Committee in relation to developing the site, giving advice, and possibly training LAA staff to their own high standards. Talks followed between senior representatives of both Charities and Wood Green expressed their willingness to help, in return for which LAA would promote the work of Wood Green. Both sides could see the potential benefits of a liaison, and the idea of Affiliation of LAA to WGAS was born. Wood Green was larger and more developed than many animal shelters and they were keen to pool their knowledge and share their expertise with smaller charities. Several members of the LAA Committee were invited to Wood Green for a look round, and they reported back to the Membership, arranging a meeting for general discussion and voting on the proposed Affiliation. The vote was positive but there were undoubtedly some mixed feelings about any kind of formal link, with concerns about takeovers, loss of identity, even loss of the name of Leicester Animal Aid. Such fears were to prove unfounded and, over the years, a very good and co-operative relationship subsequently developed. A vital link at that time was John Curzon, a member of Wood Green, elected to act as Liaison Officer between the two Charities.

Below: Newsletter announcing affiliation with WGAS and C Block

Above: Dog in an outdoor kennel and John Curzon

Below: The old incinerator

John and his colleagues gave practical advice on many matters. At the time, facilities and resources at Huncote were very poor with old, dilapidated buildings which were difficult to keep clean, and everything was being done in a very labour intensive way. The need to move the dogs in and out of the overnight accommodation every day was just one example. Another being that there was no water laid to kennel blocks and it was a daily sight to see kennel maids wheeling watering cans full of water on a wheelbarrow or rusty pram. Lack of water caused real difficulties. Wood Green sent experienced personnel to assess the best way to deal with these situations, and plans and formats were drawn up for more efficient work routines. Also LAA staff were invited to take advantage of day and residential training courses at Wood Green in order to increase their skills and generally extend their knowledge of kennel work. This was a great help. For John Curzon that initial period of consultancy developed into a much longer-term relationship, during which he served with LAA Committee effecting change and developing the site. He retains a great sense of affection for all that LAA stands for. "I have always loved Leicester Animal Aid," said John. "I like the people. I like the feel of the place. It really is a very special rescue centre, and what has been achieved in such a short space of time is just incredible."

The Committee forged ahead with its plans to bring Animal Aid into the 21st century. There were many problems to be resolved. All kennel blocks needed renewing and connecting to their own water supply and drainage, a new incinerator was needed, also new laundry facilities, including replacement washing machines and dryers, plus the house was in need of full modernisation. The plan was for all animals to have pens which gave them warmth and shelter in winter, and protection from the heat in summer – no more dogs panting in excessive heat and no more standing outside in ice or snow, being wet through when they were brought in for the night. Large exercise areas were envisaged. Hospital facilities were to be improved, and it was decided to build a modern cattery to accommodate up to 30 cats. A new administration block was needed with a Reception and waiting area, shop, education room, offices, storerooms and toilets, along with site landscaping and a new car park, so there was much to be done. Work below ground involved the total renewal of mains services, sewers, drains, cess pits, etc, causing many headaches for Committee members whose interests were in animal welfare NOT sewers and cess pits! However, as an integral part of upgrading conditions for both animals and staff, it had to be done.

Information was gathered and site plans drawn up for consideration. It was a mammoth task. Building began in the 1990s, and was continued by subsequent Committees over the years, remaining true to the concepts and visions of the original Committee, to provide all animals coming to LAA in future years with a loving 'Home' where they would be comfortably housed, and much loved. The initiatives taken then culminated in the present site, the fulfilment of a vision and an animal sanctuary to be proud of in the 21st century.

Above: The old puppy block

At the same time as plans were being made to improve the animal accommodation, the Committee gave much time and thought to improving the welfare of the animals and putting ideas and standards of care on a more formal footing, creating an Animal Welfare Policy to ensure that Animal Aid residents got the best of care from both staff and volunteers. Pat Bass recalls: "We wanted welfare standards to be 'second to none', just as good as the care we would give our own animals at home."

The Welfare Policy, agreed by the Committee in November 1993, covered all aspects of care. It is as valid today as it was then. "The welfare of the dogs who come to us for sanctuary is of paramount importance and it cannot be emphasised too strongly that all staff must work within the policies laid down by the Committee to attain a high standard of care for our residents. All animals are to be treated with gentleness, love and respect." Arrangements were specified for newly admitted dogs to ensure a proper period of assessment, including any necessary veterinary care; all dogs' details to be entered on a card index and dogs to be tagged with a LAA disc; temperatures in each block should not be allowed to fall below 50°F; warm coats to be worn by the elderly and thin-coated dogs; home checks to be carried out before homing a dog, with a follow up visit within a few weeks; names of all dogs to be displayed on their pen with a brief description of the dog. Arrangements to ensure that staff were kept updated on any new dogs coming in were agreed, as well as the principle of a weekly staff meeting to share views and opinions, and give all the opportunity to discuss the dogs and any more general kennel business. A daily grooming programme was planned but not fully implemented because of lack of staff. Nevertheless a daily hands on check by staff was introduced first thing in the morning for each dog. Similarly, dog walkers were to be encouraged to report signs of illness or injury in an Accident and Illness Book. The book was to be checked daily and information acted upon. This was all based on the principle, enshrined in the Animal

Above: Don Crowther with fellow volunteers 1988

Aid Welfare Policy, that "we wish all dogs in our care to experience nothing but kindness whilst they are with us, particularly the ones for whom life has been traumatic."

Around the same time the Committee also drew up a formal policy on euthanasia. This stated a number of situations when euthanasia should be considered the kindest option. The Policy document stated that "if a dog is suffering from one or more of the conditions listed the Committee believes that it should be Association policy to administer euthanasia before the animal suffers prolonged suffering or discomfort. It is the kindest option. Our policy must be not to let terminally ill and old dogs suffer, but to allow them to depart this life in peace and with dignity. Kennel managers will be required to follow these criteria when making decisions regarding euthanasia." Quality of life was a key measure and a veterinary consultation would always be required.

Much of the credit for the vision and transformation of LAA, and the laying of foundations to take it forward as a professional rehoming centre, must be accorded to the Management Committee of the time. It wasn't always an easy task, and there were certainly times when Sue Allcock wondered what she had taken on when, after a relatively short time as a dog walker, she found herself chairing the Management Committee, and that on top of a full-time job. Apart from animal welfare, the Committee was also implementing employment structures, staff welfare and health and safety procedures. Changes in the management of the organisation were also having to be introduced to comply with the requirements of the Charity Commission.

Below: Eric Bown

Bottom: Sue Allcock (right) and Pat Bass (left)

With the appointment, in April 1994, of Sue Stoyell, as new Manager, there was the opportunity to take forward some of the initiatives planned and begin the building work. Sue was clear about what had been achieved. "It was the Management Committee members at that time, under the chairmanship of Sue Allcock, who recognised the need to change and who were brave enough and open-minded enough to embrace this new ethos. The Trustees of the time, namely Don Crowther, Pat Bass and Eric Bown, were equally committed to change and instrumental in accomplishing it. Without them we would not be where we are today."

SUE STOYELL:
FLATMATES AND BUILDING BLOCKS

The Committee had the vision to take
LAA forward into the new Millenium.
Sharing that vision and helping to
implement it was the challenge for the
new manager. Busy times lay ahead!

Above: Old A block with dog walkers and dog in wire run

Below: Hector outside Farndon House

A period of instability had followed the retirement of Joyce and Don Kelley at the end of 1993. Finding the right manager was critical. With a background in recruitment and close links with Wood Green Animal Shelters, Sue Stoyell combined a great love of animals with a good business head. It was what was needed to take Leicester Animal Aid forward into its biggest period of expansion. Sue joined LAA in April 1994 and quickly realised there was a lot of work to be done.

"Thinking back on the way things were ten years ago when I joined LAA" says Sue, "I recall the rows of wire pens, the cement ground broken up and staff attacking the cracks with little knives endeavouring to arrest the weeds which persistently poked through. The old Blocks (A, B and C) had clearly had their day. They were not maintainable and, as they were constructed largely of wood, did not meet present day regulations. Of the three old blocks only C block had any form of drainage system.

On my arrival in the spring of '94 only A and C blocks, and the hospital, were in use. B Block was being used for storage and the boarding block, having recently been refurbished, was poised for reopening.

"Just before I joined, John Curzon and Jackie Thorburn from Wood Green Animal Shelters had paid several consultancy visits to LAA, providing invaluable input on the changes that could be made to improve methods and tidy up the site. This all paved the way for a new manager to take things forward to meet the brief of finding more homes for more dogs, and relaunching the boarding kennels. This meant a review and changes to the kennel regime and also the homing systems and methods. More had to be introduced by way of PR so that more people knew about us, and more urgent attention given to Health and Safety procedures to ensure the safety of an increasing number of visitors, not to mention staff and site volunteers."

These were daunting times and Sue soon realised she would have her hands full. Within a few weeks of her arrival the first litter of pups had taken up residence in her flat. Sleepy, Bashful, Nicki and Smiley, Collie X pups, were only about three weeks old when they came to stay before going on to be rehomed. Then on lst May that year a little scrap of a pup, aged about six weeks, was picked up in a field. By then Sue had already had two litters in her bathroom and didn't really fancy any more puddles on the floor for a while. But, of course, she took the pup in. He was named Hector and never did leave! Over the years Hector, helped out by Rosie the cat, has taken under his wing an endless string of puppies, kittens, older dogs and cats, all of whom at some point have had to be taken into the flat for some tender loving care.

There were no cats on site when Sue arrived, although that soon began to change and and it wasn't long before litters of kittens took up residence in Sue's bathroom. Soon the cats were to become as much a part of the family as the dogs.

With no proper office base, it was hard to see how anything would be sorted. Certainly trying to run LAA from the flat was not going to work. The arrival of two portakabins which would serve as a Reception and Office was a massive boost. These were duly equipped with a photocopier, typewriter and fax machine which Sue had brought with her, and provided an essential base on site.

Above: Rosie whispering to Hector

Below: The first portakabin arriving and the old boarding block – later changed to intake

Christmas that year brought one of Sue's more unusual phone calls - from a lady reporting a stray ostrich in her back garden! It was Christmas Eve, dark, and blowing a gale, and that evening the RSPCA were unable to help immediately. Clearly the tactics used to round up a stray dog would not be much use. Fortunately the Yellow Pages revealed a nearby ostrich farm, and the escapee was duly rounded up and taken away by the farmer.

Soon after Sue's arrival B Block was opened to take new intake animals, thus increasing capacity from about 40 to 55 dogs. The boarding service had been refurbished to meet all regulatory requirements and the service got off to a good start; by the second year it was fully booked in summer and during bank holidays. Although the boarding kennels brought in useful income, there were issues about combining a boarding service and rescue centre on one site. For a start the blocks were too close to each other, with a real danger of cross infection. It was impossible to be in two places at once: owners calling to deposit or collect their dog for boarding invariably arrived at the same time that a traumatised new rescue dog was being brought in. And then there were the real problems! The worry as owners returned to collect their dogs only to find that Fido's treasured squeaky toy had rolled under the wire and was the object of

Above: Podge the Greyhound

Below: Lenney the greyhound in the old quarters amd Marion Turner with Greyhound, Harvey

great attention for the dog next door. Or the insistence that Fido had to have a cup of tea and a biscuit at 6 o'clock every evening. And of course occasions when 'mummy and daddy' expected a postcard from their cherished pet! So Sue would often find herself sitting in the boarding block at 11 o'clock at night, pandering to one of the boarders.

It was all too much and in late 1996 it was decided that the boarding service should be discontinued in favour of taking in more rescue dogs. There was a long waiting list of animals needing to come in but there was a need to make up the lost revenue from boarding in other ways. Shortly afterwards LAA took on the stray contracts for Blaby and Oadby and Wigston District Councils, an arrangement which has continued to this day and fits much better with the overall ethos of the Centre.

Discontinuing the boarding function allowed the boarding block to be brought into service as an isolation intake facility, greatly improving intake procedures. All dogs were able to spend necessary quiet time in the intake area where they were handled by only a few people who they came to know and trust. All the dogs were health checked, vaccinated, neutered and assessed. Staff were better able to assess each dog's homing requirements, thereby ensuring they had the best possible chance of a happy new start in life.

By the time Sue arrived there was a sound welfare policy in place which included the vaccination and neutering of the animals. This meant weekly visits from the Veterinary Surgeon. This inevitably resulted in increased overheads which necessitated a new concentration on marketing and extra energy put into fund raising. People responded magnificently. The old site shop was taken in hand again by a keen team of regular jumble sorters which resulted in a thriving little Aladdin's cave, regular auctions, site sales, car boot sales and regular attendance at outside events where there were opportunities to sell bric a brac, clothes etc. In order to launch a new range of promotional goods a distinctive new logo was designed. In addition, Marian Turner, Fundraising Administrator, was appointed in January 1998 to complete the team.

The challenge presented to Sue on arrival was to turn an animal sanctuary into a rehoming centre. On the homing side LAA was became increasingly successful with more professional assessments of the dogs, more thorough interviewing of those offering prospective homes and a home checking system by a committed team of volunteers. As Sue says: "There is no precise science in the successful homing of dogs but LAA does have a good reputation for getting the match right. Since the very beginning LAA has been noted for caring about the animals both before and after they have been homed. This feeling of family has stayed with us and must continue to lie at the core of everything we do."

LAA was, however, facing a major challenge. The necessity to rebuild the animal housing was not going to go away. A Business Plan was essential to provide the focus that was needed for the next 6 years. It was important to bring the rescue dogs' accommodation up to as high a standard as possible. At that time John Rogers, professional kennel designer and builder, came on the scene. He put up a proposed site plan which was duly accepted in outline by the Management Committee, though to most the plan represented a dim and distant dream. At the AGM on 27 March 1994, however, the capital expenditure was agreed and the plan approved.

February 1995 saw a planning application for the first new kennel block submitted. This was to be part of a complete £300,000 overhaul of the entire site, involving demolition of outbuildings and outdated kennels, and replacement with modern facilities. There was much debate about how to proceed in order to ensure the overall layout was attractive to visitors and easy for staff to work in but, most importantly, provided the right standard of accommodation for the rescue animals.

With a donation of £5,000 from the Helen Jean Cope Trust, the first part of the refurbishment focused on the hospital block. The hospital was officially opened at Open Day in the summer of 1996 and was very quickly put to use with a litter of puppies and various other older pups coming in for rehoming.

In the summer of 1997 detailed plans for the whole site were drawn up, building regulations obtained, and planning permission granted. In order to fund the rebuilding work, a massive fund raising appeal – the Huncote Hounds Millenium Appeal – was duly launched in order to raise the £300,000 needed. Former LAA resident, Max, the greyhound, became the Appeal mascot, making guest appearances at fund-raising events and inviting animal lovers to 'buy a brick' in support of the rebuilding.

There was an urgent need to start work on rebuilding one of the kennel blocks at an estimated cost of around £50-60,000. At that point LAA

Above: The LAA new logo

Below: Newsletter Summer 1996 – Refurbishment Project: proposed development and Newsletter Spring 1998 – work begins on new kennel block: Janet Campion and John Rogers photo

Above: Work on site – Marion Turner, with LAA dog, Sally

Below: Hector and flatmate, Hero (top) and Joey (bottom)

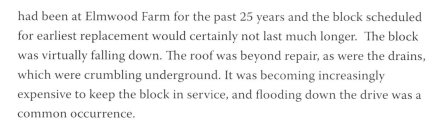

had been at Elmwood Farm for the past 25 years and the block scheduled for earliest replacement would certainly not last much longer. The block was virtually falling down. The roof was beyond repair, as were the drains, which were crumbling underground. It was becoming increasingly expensive to keep the block in service, and flooding down the drive was a common occurrence.

Work on that first new block began with the laying of the foundations in February 1998 – the start of a new era for LAA. In charge of design and construction was Shrewsbury company, Rogers and Associates Ltd, specialists in kennel construction. Managing Director, John Rogers, revealed there was far more to the task than just stacking bricks. "Great thought goes into the design for maximum comfort, cleanliness and practicality," he said. "One of the great concerns is sound reduction. The special roofing material gives protection against heatstroke in summer. Every pen has a pop hole so each dog can decide whether it wants to be inside or out in its run. The improved ease of cleaning the new facilities will make a huge difference to staff. Panels between runs can be changed from mesh to solid plastic to suit the individual dog's temperament, whether they enjoy a friend next door, or suffer from kennel stress."

For staff and volunteers alike, these were exciting times. The block had its own kitchen and a sluice, which meant staff no longer had to cart mucky buckets across the site. With double glazed windows, extractor fans and gas heating, the new block provided a wonderfully cosy and comfortable home for the lucky little dogs. This block, later to be named Farndon Block, was opened on Open Day in June 1998, and set the standard of accommodation for all dogs in the care of LAA. The challenge then was to raise more money so that other new blocks could follow.

By way of distraction from building work, Sue found herself with a steady stream of flatmates over the years, all needing a bit of extra love and attention. Little Joey, a Jack Russell X pup was brought in at 6 weeks old having been rescued from a railway line. A cheeky young pup, Joey remained quite a handful even as he got older, but a real charmer nonetheless. Honey, a Collie X, had two visits to the flat, the last at

Above: Another flatmate, Honey

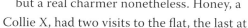

the age of eleven, before going on to a wonderful foster home where she spent the rest of her days. Hero, a pup, came in to LAA at 8 weeks of age suffering from parvo virus and abandoned. After a period in isolation, he enjoyed a period of convalescence in the flat. Grommit, too, an elderly terrier prone to fits found friends in Hector and Rosie, staying in the flat for several weeks. Undoubtedly the youngest pups to take up residence in the flat were Teddy, Bengey, Eddy and Spider. They came in at one day old when their mother died shortly after their birth. Sue, Hector and Rosie took care of them in the early weeks, together with LAA volunteer, Lesley Dawes-Gamble. There were a few anxious times in the early days but all four pups flourished and grew up to be happy, healthy and extremely handsome dogs, all finding homes without any trouble.

Meanwhile, plans for the next new block had already been drawn up. All that was needed were the funds to go ahead. With perfect timing, the rebuilding project received a major boost with the announcement of a £110,000 windfall from a benevolent fund. Following a visit to LAA by a Mrs Murphy, Trustees of the Edith Murphy Foundation, a Leicester based charity, decided to donate the entire costs of a brand new state of the art kennel block. This new block would provide 20 pens and runs for larger breeds of dogs. Work started in October 1999 and it was a proud moment at Open Day the following year when the second new block in the redevelopment project, the Edith Murphy Foundation Kennel Block, was opened by David Tams, one of the Trustees.

Above: Grommit and basket of pups Teddy, Bengey, Eddy and Spider

Above: David Tams, Don Crowther and Sue Stoyell – opening of Edith Murphy Foundation Block.

Sanctuary dogs: Scamper

Big Sue

Sadie

Oscar

Once the Murphy Block was completed, attention then moved to plans for a third new kennel block for the longer stay dogs, the sanctuary dogs who, for one reason or another, often behavioural problems, were likely to be at LAA for a long time. Plans for them included new pens, but also separate play areas overlooking the large paddock. The sanctuary dogs hold a special place in the hearts of all who come to know them. Four in residence when Sue joined LAA are remembered with particular affection. Scamper, the lurcher, always a big personality on site and who died at LAA some two years after Sue's arrival a very old fellow. Big Sue, a border collie, was elderly and diabetic, needing insulin injections every day, but lived on for several more years, a great favourite and sadly missed when she eventually died. Oscar was definitely the boss on site, assuming the responsibilities of a sergeant major carefully inspecting each kennel and bed before dismissing the kennel assistant on duty. A wonderful dog, Oscar died in 1995. Lastly, Sadie, a real sanctuary favourite, who died in late 2004. Sadie was something of a mascot. Somewhat choosy about the human company she kept, nevertheless a great favourite with staff and (some) dog walkers! "Lovely when she gets to know you," is how Sadie is best remembered.

But back to the building work! It was not just the kennels that were undergoing refurbishment. The somewhat grandly named Education Centre had been created when the old dogs' kitchen was divided. Refurbishment was carried out with funds raised by Year 9 of Heathfield School and the Lorraine Charity Trust. Not large, but the centre did provide a useful venue for meetings, and also talks and group visits.

September 2001 saw yet another part of the jigsaw fall into place with the opening of the new cattery, designed to ensure that cats as well as dogs were housed in the best possible environment.

By the autumn of 2001 it was time to sit back and reflect on all the changes. Looking at the purpose designed dog kennelling (Farndon, Murphy and Sanctuary Blocks), the turfed play areas for the dogs and the newly built Cattery, it was clear that the vision of four years ago had become a reality.

Almost the last part of the jigsaw, as far as the dogs were concerned, was the building of the new intake block. Dale Neal from Radio Leicester formally opened the new intake block on Open Day 2003, joining

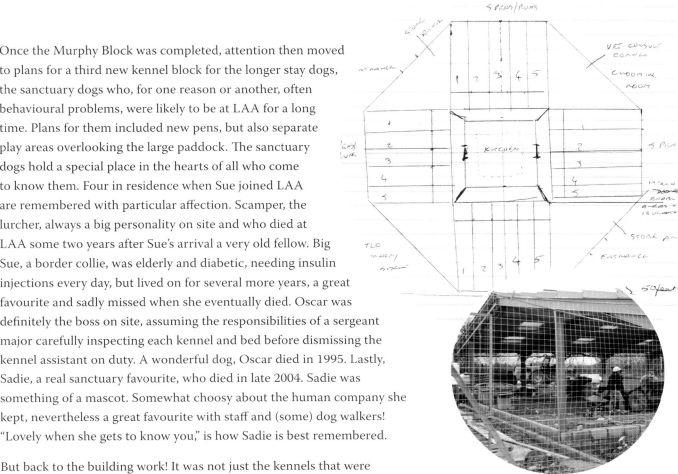

Above: Sue Stoyell drawing of proposed new intake block and construction under way on the intake block

Below: Dale Neal from Radio Leicester cutting the ribbon at the opening of the intake block

Above: Sue Stoyell and Janet Campion

Below: Sue Stoyell and Edith Murphy at Sue's retirement

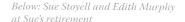

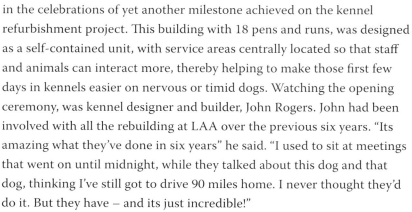

in the celebrations of yet another milestone achieved on the kennel refurbishment project. This building with 18 pens and runs, was designed as a self-contained unit, with service areas centrally located so that staff and animals can interact more, thereby helping to make those first few days in kennels easier on nervous or timid dogs. Watching the opening ceremony, was kennel designer and builder, John Rogers. John had been involved with all the rebuilding at LAA over the previous six years. "Its amazing what they've done in six years" he said. "I used to sit at meetings that went on until midnight, while they talked about this dog and that dog, thinking I've still got to drive 90 miles home. I never thought they'd do it. But they have – and its just incredible!"

The final kennel building project, completed early in 2004, was the extension to the Hospital Block, involving a summer house for the elderly dogs to enjoy and a porch running the length of the building.

While all this building work was going on, the site was also undergoing something of a transformation. The rose garden had originally been donated by Committee member, Miss Garvey, in memory of her niece. The beds were lovingly restored in the mid 1990s by volunteer, Beryl Bloxham. It remains a peaceful spot, with dedications to the memory of lost pets, many of the roses being donated by dog walkers when old favourites passed away. There had been no burials in the cemetery for at least ten years and this was transformed into a wildlife garden, full of donated bee, bird and butterfly friendly plants. The paddock adjoining the kennels was planted as a copse to encourage wildlife and adds to the facilities on offer particularly for group tours. With a newly erected hide and well stocked bird feeders, this area has become a haven for wildlife, continuing the conservation theme that is an important feature of the work of LAA.

With the needs of the animals taken care of, it was clearly time to turn the focus on the needs of staff and visitors, with a new Education and Visitor Centre to include reception, offices, shop and refreshment facilities. The temporary portakabin facilities had certainly run their course. Although not complete, it was entirely appropriate that Sue Stoyell's 'retirement do', on 21st November 2004, was the first official event to be held in the new building. Worries on Sue's part that no-one would turn up on a miserable Sunday afternoon in November proved completely unfounded. The room was packed with friends new and old, keen to acknowledge all that had been achieved during Sue's ten years at the helm, and her key role in those achievements, and equally to wish her, and of course Hector, well in retirement.

As she contemplated retirement after an amazing decade with LAA, Sue Stoyell reflected on all that had been achieved. "It has been a progressive few years with many animals homed – around 5,000 and this is what it has all been about. It is they alone that have provided the motivation and commitment for us to move ahead. When I say "us" I mean people who have served on management committees and sub-committees, staff, supporters and volunteers, not forgetting the three original Trustees namely Pat Bass, Eric Bown, and the late Don Crowther. I will always be grateful to Don for his sound advice and encouragement and his sudden death was a tragic loss to us all. He chaired the original Marketing Committee and was responsible for a lot of good work in this area. LAA inspires huge commitment from everyone involved, and I have been fortunate in the staff I have worked with, and particularly in the superb guidance and support from two Chairpeople, firstly Sue Allcock and, for most of my time as manager, Janet Campian.

"I shall miss everything about LAA, but I leave feeling that it has been a huge privilege to have been part of LAA at such an exciting time in its history. A new management team is in place. The Education and Visitor Centre will open up all kinds of opportunities. I leave with rich memories, many happy and even funny, but inevitably some that are sad for those we could not save or help. Finally, I have much to thank LAA for and top of my list is my wonderful dog, Hector, and for little Rosie my cat. They have both shared with me some wonderful, if not hectic years at LAA. Retirement will mean me having more time to spend with them."

Above: Baby blackbird – another of Sue's rescues

Below: Murphy, another of the flatmates

57

VOLUNTEERS:
'THE UNSUNG HEROES'

A huge part of the success of Leicester Animal Aid is down to the "unsung heroes" – the hundreds of volunteers and supporters, far too many to name, but who over the years have given unstinting service in so many different ways.

In the early days of LAA, before there were any paid staff, volunteers were the lifeblood which kept the organisation going. Fifty years on LAA might have grown, and there are now paid staff, but still the reliance on the loyal army of supporters, who help out in so many, and such diverse, ways is as strong as ever. So many people have given, and continue to give, generously of their time, that it is impossible to name them all. Whoever they are, whatever they might have done, and whatever they may do in the future, we are grateful to them all: LAA would not be the same without their loyalty and their help.

One of the very first volunteers was Archibald Smith. He began by helping Mrs Farndon at Thurmaston Lane, and subsequently becoming Patron of LAA in the late 1970s. A retired company executive, he would spend at least 2 days a week at the kennels, exercising around 50 dogs. He was an avid dog lover. His own dog, Rufus, was an LAA pup, whose mother, Jill, a tiny terrier, was found starving, and later died giving birth to her pups. His wife, Irene, helped run a stall selling rummage on Leicester Market until a shop was opened for this purpose. At the time of his death in November 1998, aged 84, Archibald Smith had been a Trustee and helper for over 40 years. He is remembered by many as a champion dog walker: until well into his seventies, he still spent at least one day a week at the kennels, taking about 20 dogs for walks.

Above: Archibald Smith with Lassie

Left: Information for Volunteers leaflet

Fund raising has always been a major challenge and relies hugely on the loyal band of supporters. On numerous occasions over the years there have been concerns about how much longer the organisation could keep going. With crisis appeals launched, somehow the necessary injection of cash would come just in time. The running costs continue to rise. In 1971 they were about £70 a week, in 1975 over £200, and by 1984 £500 a week. By 1995 costs had risen to £7,500 a month, going up to £12,000 a month in 1999, £15,000 a month in 2002, and by 2005 had reached £26,000 a month. These sums take a huge effort to raise.

Throughout the LAA year there are a number of important fund raising events – Open Day, Family Fun Day, the annual raffle, mini-markets, the Christmas Bazaar and Auction. Open Day 1997

Above and right: Fundraising auction

Above: Christmas Bazaar 2002 and Open Day stalls

saw a fund raising event with a difference when a friendly band of Vikings set up camp on the bottom field. They caused quite a stir when they sent a raiding party to capture a few "natives", one of which was LAA Chair, Janet Campion. At the end of the day an auction of the captives was held, with all proceeds from the raid going to support LAA. Rumour has it that Janet's husband had to bid heavily to ensure her safe return. The weather is not always kind on these occasions, and a fair few Open Days have seen the paddocks turn into a quagmire, but it doesn't stop the loyal band of supporters who turn out to help man the stalls and those who visit on the day, the bric-a-brac stalls always proving a great attraction, however damp the items for sale. The Midland Bernese Carters are always a popular attraction and great supporters of LAA.

Below: Midland Bernese Carters at Open Day 2005 and Sponsored head shave

Over the years there have been a million and one ways that individuals or groups have helped by raising funds. There have been sponsored walks, runs, slims, head shaves, silences, Games Days, fashion shows, and pub crawls. One local pub sold dog chews over the bar. Another had a swear box on the bar. One man apparently put £1 in the box every time he came into the pub to get in credit for when he did swear! Donations have been given instead of Christmas cards. One local dog grooming salon donated proceeds from clipping dogs nails over the previous 12 months. Others have abseiled over the side of local buildings or flung themselves from aeroplanes for sponsored parachute jumps. In 1998, volunteer, Jan Smith, organised a fund raising concert, managing to bring together eleven former D'Oyly Carte principals, backed by a chorus drawn from the leading singers in several Leicester musical groups. People travelled from all over the country for what was a fabulous evening, and a very significant fund raiser.

A regular fundraising event for many years was the Sponsored Walk, an ideal opportunity for a nice stroll in the countryside, and a good chance for canine friends to take part too. Of course, the weather was fairly

Leicester & Leicestershire Animal Aid Association

HUNCOTE HOUND MILLENNIUM APPEAL

Gala Evening

of

GILBERT & SULLIVAN FAVOURITES

Featuring former D'Oyly Carte Principals

SATURDAY 22 AUGUST 1998
"Y" THEATRE,
EAST STREET, LEICESTER

Above: Programme for Gilbert and Sullivan Concert

Below: Help with the food stocks

critical: too hot and no-one wants to walk very far. And then sometimes it can be too wet! The walk in September 2000 was probably one of the wettest days of the decade, but still a few stalwarts ventured out to complete the course, even though by the end it was more like a sponsored paddle than walk.

LAA has been immensely fortunate over the years in the support it has received from legacies – sometimes from people who have had a dog from LAA at some point or had been involved in some other way, but not necessarily so. The income from legacies is vital in supplementing normal income and enabling LAA to move forward with the amazing programme of capital expansion that we have seen in recent years.

Support for LAA comes in numerous ways. There are shops that take collecting tins, and individuals who willingly go out to collect them when they are full. Some shops have a bin to collect donations of food from customers, but these also rely on volunteers to collect the food. Then there are the regular street collections. It is always a fact that the size of the collection is higher if one of the collectors has a dog with them. Unfortunately, nowadays, particularly when the collection takes place outside a supermarket, it is not always possible for a dog to go along and help. So, Sue Stoyell hit on the idea of the next best thing – a life size cardboard cut out of a dog. It certainly helps to draw the crowds!

The LAA rose garden had become totally overgrown when Beryl Bloxham wandered up to Sue Stoyell who was obviously struggling and asked if she would like some help with the garden. So Beryl took it on, transforming it from its overgrown state into what it is today. Like many volunteers, she later took on Millie, a lurcher, and continues to be a valuable member of the Wednesday team that sorts all the donated goods each week.

Help with the huge food bill is always much appreciated. An event with a difference is the annual food dash by the British Motorcycle Federation. This event, which started in 1996, sees a large number of leather-clad bikers dashing round the country each year collecting food, and finishing up at LAA with a veritable mountain of goodies. The Motor Cycle Club of local firm, Caterpillar, have also done regular food runs over the years.

Being known as "the bag lady" may not suit everyone, but for Edna Lines it is certainly a very appropriate label. Her deep tan is a testament to the miles she walks as one of the team of devoted dog walkers. With a keen eye on fundraising possibilities, however, Edna also has a constant stream of items for sale. She chuckles as she recalls that friends have been known to see her coming and duck behind the nearest bush, while her family know that visits always result in some high pressure selling. One friend apparently said of the haircut Edna used to give him: "It wasn't cheap given that I had to buy a pair of trousers and a shirt to go with it!" For Edna its just all part of her tireless efforts over many years in support of LAA.

Above: British Motor Cycle Federation food dash

Perhaps the most visible of the volunteers are the dog walkers. Whatever the weather they are out in force. Striding along the road, now resplendent in their luminous yellow jackets, courtesy of Acresford Sand and Gravel, they tred a well-beaten path. Arriving at the kennels at Huncote in torrential rain, it is tempting to sit it out in the car and wait for the rain to pass. The volunteer dog walkers are made of sterner stuff. There are times when it is hard to say who looks more like a drowned rat – the dog walker or the dog!

Below: Edna Lines at Open Day 2005

Seeing the dogs lining up for their walks, and the dog walkers going out time after time, it is hard to imagine a time when the dogs were not regularly walked, but that was certainly the case, in April 1982, when Pat Bass first visited LAA. At that point there were approximately 90 dogs in residence and out of that number, only a small number of dogs were walked at weekends – by Jean and Ken Oliver, Ros, Rita, and other volunteers. Apart from Mr Smith's small group in the week, the rest never went out.

Pat had just lost a much-loved dog when she visited LAA kennels for the first time. She asked if she could take some dogs for a walk to help her get over the loss of her own dog, and also to help out. Offers of help are never turned down and Joyce Kelley, LAA Manager at the time, very quickly agreed. So one afternoon, Pat took Scamp for a walk up the lane. When she came back and put him in his pen next to Bruce, she decided she couldn't go away and leave Bruce, so Bruce became her second dog. Everyone entering or leaving LAA at that time had to pass Dogsey, a staffie X who 'lived' in a kennel by the gate. He was on a long chain as he was a renowned escapologist, and no pen had ever contained him for long. Dogsey watched her go in and out with Bruce and Scamp so, when she brought Bruce back, she took Dogsey out! Snowy,

Perry, Penny and Lexi (the oldest resident at 20 years of age) watched wistfully as Dogsey was put back on his chain after his walk. Pat couldn't leave them so the five of them went down the field, along with the two donkeys, Jubilee and Pippin.

For Pat that afternoon had a huge impact. "I went home and thought – long and hard. I couldn't bear to think of all those dogs shut up in their kennels for weeks, months or, in many cases, years. Some were institutionalised, some were of uncertain temperament, others were gentle and affectionate. All needed someone to give them individual attention so I decided to take more of them out."

Pat started going to the kennels 3 or 4 times a week for many hours. She would put one dog in the bottom field, one in the side, one in the top field, whilst she took another dog for a walk – thus getting four at a time out of their sterile environment. Then all of the dogs from the hospital were taken out to potter around the fields together. In this way she was able to take out between 24 and 30 dogs each time she visited, making sure the next time that she took out those who'd missed out before.

Above: Dog walkers

Below: Bruce

Bottom: Penny, Snowy and Perry

For Pat it was heartbreaking to see eager dogs coming towards their door and having to say, "Sorry, not today." Sitting at home she worried about the dogs who weren't being walked. Something had to be done but help was needed. And so the idea of the Dog Walking Scheme was born. Posters were prepared – 'Dog Walkers Wanted' - and these were placed on notice boards throughout the county, in libraries, in shops, in supermarkets and, sure enough, little by little, people responded. Joyce Kelley was happy for Pat to go ahead providing she organised things properly, and ensured the suitability of the walkers and the safety of the dogs. So Pat insisted on personally meeting each new walker and "vetting" them, and also introducing them to suitable dogs to walk. A notice board was put up with information regarding safety procedures. A plan of the kennels was painted on an old blackboard. Pat wrote each dog's name in the appropriate place so that it could be found easily, and had name plates put on all the kennels. These served two purposes. Firstly, walkers could find 'their' dog, and, secondly, visitors could call the dog by name, so helping to give the dogs an individual identity. When walkers had taken a dog out they ticked its name on the blackboard so that each day it was possible to see which dogs had gone out.

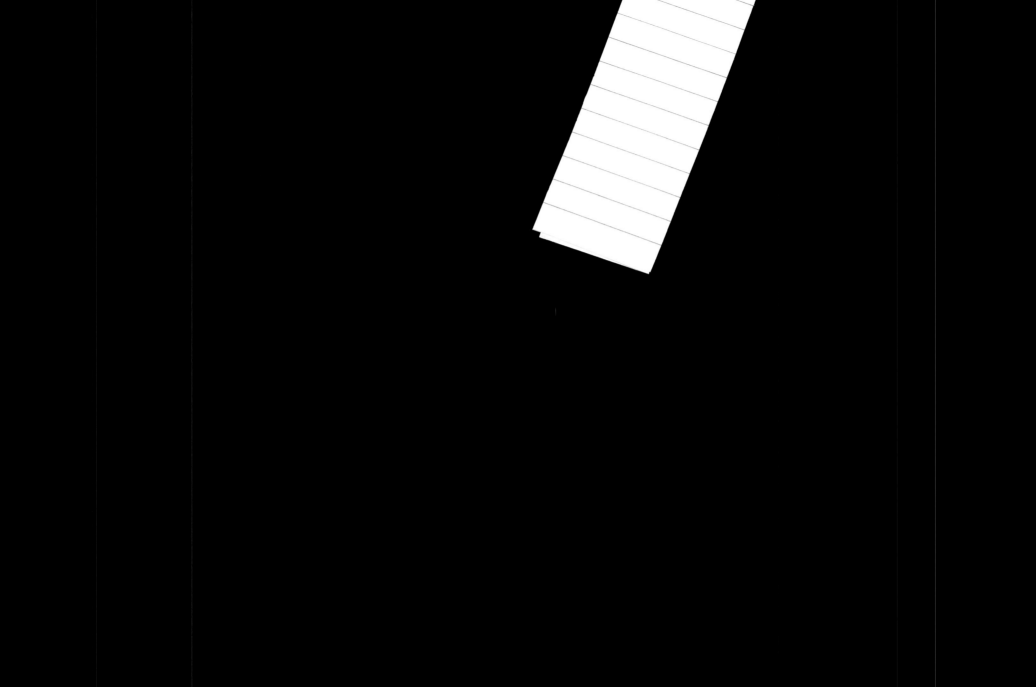

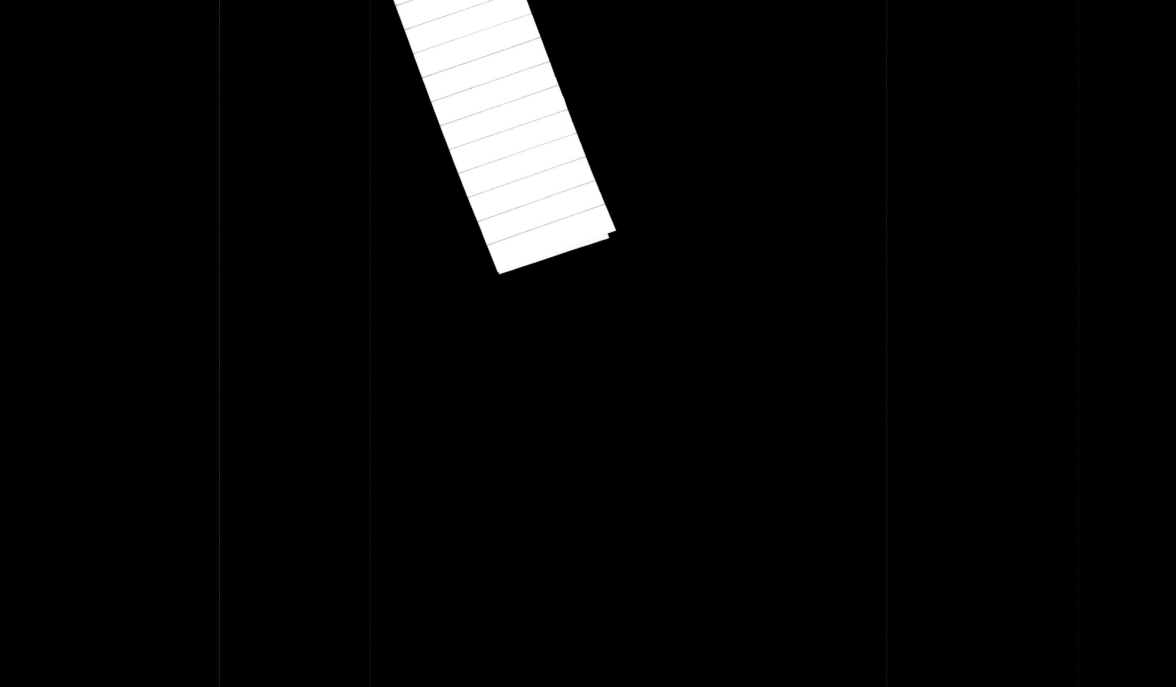

"The first years were very difficult as so many walkers came and went in rapid succession" recalls Pat. "However, bit by bit, a nucleus of good, reliable people stayed with us and became deeply involved. Each walker was allocated a group of dogs to take out until we reached the first goal. Every dog in the kennels was getting one walk a week. We persevered with advertising. More people came. Goal two was reached. Every dog was getting out twice a week. At that time my husband, Trevor, was helping. He took out the 'difficult' dogs, and there were quite a number – Nigger, Sam, Squirt, George, Little Scamp, Rex, Piper, Midge and Roly come to mind. They were quite a handful. I also took them out and closely vetted any dog walkers who were prepared to take their chance! Eventually a group of stalwarts was formed to take on these 'difficult dogs' so they too went out regularly and, in most cases, their behaviour was much improved.

"Over a number of years a wonderfully loyal and loving group of walkers became the backbone of the whole dog walking scheme. It took five years of hard work before we reached our final goal of every dog getting out every day, and there was much rejoicing when that was achieved. That was some 16 years ago and since then every dog has been walked every day, thanks to a fantastic team of dog lovers who have braved ice, snow, wind, rain, hail and heat to walk 'their' dogs, never letting them down. These people have done wonders for the dogs, transforming the lives of the dogs in care, particularly the long-stay dogs. They have given so much more than the walks – one to one attention and love. Dog walkers (over 50 of them each week making up the team) have also supported Leicester Animal Aid in so many other ways, and many of them have given loving homes to our residents – the old ones in particular."

Pat is in no doubt where the credit for the success of the dog walking scheme lies. "I can claim to have started the scheme but credit must go to the hundreds of walkers over the past 21 years who have kept it going. The dogs are lucky to have so many very good friends."

It is not only the dogs who gain from the Dog Walking Scheme. Writing in the Christmas 1996 LAA Newsletter, Eric Bown reflects on how his involvement with LAA began. "Many years ago, I had just gone through the pain and anguish of losing my beloved Springer Spaniel, Ben. Taking a walk without a dog was just not the same. At the same time I wasn't sure I could go through the trauma of losing another dog, so my wife suggested that I try dog walking at LAA. This was around

Above: Notices on kennels and Ken Oliver sorting the dog walking rota

Bottom: Little Scamp and George

Above: Doreen Laker with Bugsie, and dog walker Karen Fall with Twirley

Below: Dog walkers Christmas party

the time that Pat Bass was almost single-handedly trying to organise a scheme whereby each dog would be given at least one walk a day. Often we didn't have enough walkers to achieve this, no matter how hard we tried but over the years many people have given great service to the dogs and the kennels. For me, personally, walking the dogs has been a source of great satisfaction. It has also been a chance to meet and enjoy the company of many like-minded people. What pleases me particularly is just how many of the walkers have met and fallen in love with a kennel dog and given that dog a new home." Needless to say more than one LAA resident has found its way into Eric's home! Bugsie was another whose poor start had a happy ending with other dog walkers. Unwanted and turned out into the street before being taken to LAA by neighbours, Bugsie was certainly very neglected but not daunted in spirit, he was a comical little dog who quickly won the hearts of LAA supporters, Doreen and Frank Laker.

For Viv Crowther, another LAA stalwart, dog walking took on a different meaning. It was Open Day 1984 when she first visited Huncote. A strategically placed notice on one of the kennels was to be the start of a long and happy involvement with LAA. "This dog needs a cuddle." This was the captivating message from Dinky, son of two well known Huncote residents, Dogsey and Peggy. Viv was not well so couldn't walk the dogs so she took on the task of caring for "the old, the nasty and the dying". If they couldn't walk far, that was no problem. Viv would just load the dogs into a wheelbarrow, sometimes several at a time, and wheel them down to the field, so that they could just potter about gently.

Some home comforts were soon to follow. Viv's mother, donated a garden shed in memory of her husband. Erected in what was then known as 'Viv's field' – now the main car park, this was no ordinary shed. For a start it was carpeted, it was also heated. At Christmas there was even a Christmas tree. The walls were adorned with poems, written by Viv in memory of some of the Huncote residents who had died. One Boxing Day, Viv found herself sharing the shed with a total of eleven dogs. Not surprisingly, she sometimes had to fend off the dog walkers who would often find their way to the shed just to have a warm.

When Shirley Campbell, another long-time dog walker and supporter of LAA, died in September 2003, a jig - The Huncote Jig - was arranged in her memory. Performed at Open Day 2004, the jig was dedicated to "that band of volunteers who brave the elements – the dog walkers".

The home check scheme is equally reliant on volunteers – the home checkers, an amazing band of people ever ready to respond to home check requests in a matter of hours, sometimes travelling to far flung places around the country in pursuit of suitable new homes for LAA dogs. Viv Crowther was one of the first official home checkers. Some home checks were carried out before dogs were homed, but then Joyce Kelley would say: "Viv, I'm a bit worried about this one, do you think you could just pop round and make sure everything is OK." So the process of follow up visits was initiated. The records of those early home visits are recorded for posterity in a series of "dog-eared" exercise books. Together with the dog walking scheme, the introduction of the formal home check scheme really did mark a turning point for LAA.

Then there are those who foster elderly dogs and cats. The foster scheme, introduced in 1994, was aimed at providing foster homes for the elderly and frail dogs who would benefit from a home environment, but might not otherwise find a home. With this scheme, Leicester Animal Aid maintains responsibility for all veterinary bills and decisions, whilst providing fosterers with continual support.

The first dog to benefit from this scheme was Ben. He responded very well under the scheme and this encouraged them to try with other dogs. Shep, a lovely old German Shepherd, who had severe muscle wastage responded well to lots of TLC from his foster owners, not to mention a warm place by the fireside. He amazed everyone by his ability to walk half a mile a day with his foster owners. Another dog, Bess, one of the kennel favourites, a dignified and very gracious old lady of a collie had a lovely life in her foster home, being spoilt rotten by her foster owners. Mac, another old favourite, a white lurcher with black patches, was fostered to a long-standing dog walker, ensuring that he would find the love and comfort he so deserved for the rest of his days.

The foster scheme relies not only on good cooperation between fosterers and the kennels, but also on the generosity and kindness of fosterers in taking dogs with special needs into their homes. In Spring 2003 a total of 40 animals were in homes under the foster scheme. While the scheme is very costly to LAA, it does ensure that older animals get to enjoy their twilight years enjoying the comforts of a home, with a loving foster 'mum or dad' to take care of them.

Above: Dancers doing the 'Huncote Jig'

Below: Foster dogs, Ben and Thomas, waiting for vet consultation

Above: Don Crowther

Below: Dana Newcombe with Robbie

Above: Pam England with dog, Jackie

Committee membership may not be everyone's choice but, as with all things, LAA is hugely reliant on volunteers to support the various Committees, including Management and Marketing. Over the years a large number of people have given their time to sit on committees, and to help shape the policies and strategy for LAA, to serve as Trustees or in other positions. The sudden death of Don Crowther in April 2003 was a source of great sadness for all who knew him, and a major loss to LAA. Don had been an enthusiastic and influential supporter of LAA for many years. He became a Senior Trustee in 1991, at a time when the Charity was under very real threat of closure. Without Don's businesslike approach to LAA, the outcome at that time might have been very different. It was Don and the other Senior Trustees who provided the focus for moving the Charity forward, modernising the constitution and the management structure. Talking in 1995 to Monica Winfield of Radio Leicester on an outside broadcast from LAA Don summed up the challenge: "An organisation like Animal Aid can either go forward or it goes backwards, there's no standing still. And we must go forward, and we will." Don steered the Charity's investments, ensuring a solid financial base for the major renovation programme that was entering its final stages when he died. He took on the chairmanship of the newly formed Marketing Committee – always providing an update on the latest situation regarding LAA stocks and shares and the investment world in general, and always looking to the future. LAA owes Don a huge debt.

Dana Newcombe has fulfilled virtually every role there is over the years, from dog walking, helping to man Reception, and performing just about every role on the Committee. Dana also continues to be one of the busiest home checkers. Those who have braved the sponsored walk over the years will remember her with gratitude as 'the refreshment stop'. Pam England, another loyal supporter of almost twenty years, is also known to turn her hand to support in any way that's needed. Anne Martin, has only been with LAA for six years after retiring from work. She now finds herself "working" three days a week at Huncote, dog walking, hands on kennel duties, manning reception, jumble sorting and all kinds of fund-raising. Five years ago she joined the Committee, becoming vice Chair two years later. Anne was lucky enough to have known Mrs Farndon, having visited her house on Saffron Road with jumble and other goods. "I remember the house: it was so full of cats and dogs. I'll never forget the sight of a cat walking up and down the keys of the grand piano in the lounge!"

How to get involved in LAA – without really trying? That's a question that volunteers Margaret and Tony Stokes have often asked themselves.

For Margaret, it all started with daily walks around the village when she began to get on "nodding" terms with the other dog walkers and eventually stopping for a chat. That's how she got to know Janet Campion, LAA Chair. Janet told Margaret about LAA, and particularly the problems with trying to get the organisation more up to date. To Margaret it sounded interesting but she hadn't got time to get involved. Janet also mentioned the dog walking scheme. That was something Margaret could do, but only for a couple of hours one morning a week. She even persuaded a friend to join too.

On Margaret's first day as LAA dog walker, she thought she had walked into a greyhound sanctuary – there were so many of them. Mary Dakin, head dog walker for that day, took her to see Duke – he had a slightly bent foot which made him useless for racing. Duke was very friendly with people – but hated other dogs. At that time the dogs were brought out of their sleeping quarters and into outside pens every morning. So taking Duke for a walk meant arriving early and taking him out – past the other pens - with teeth barred and lots of barking! Once past the other dogs, Duke walked calmly and serenely down the road, with Margaret having to check from time to time to make sure he was still at the end of the lead. After that lovely walk it was back again to be introduced to another greyhound and off again. The LAA journey had begun!

Above: Janet Campion and Mary Dakin with Poppy

One thing led to another. As Margaret recalls: "Eventually I became a member of LAA and one day the Secretary Sheila turned up at my door to say that the Treasurer had resigned and would I take on the job. It was a bit of a shock! I was a book-keeper and the thought of taking on the role of Treasurer was a bit daunting. I decided to look at the books – they were quite simple and it was not going to be an arduous job - so Treasurer I became. With the advent of Spons-a-dog, the brain child of Lynn Walker, for which payments are made by standing order, I started to use our computer to help manage the accounts." Later, husband Tony got caught up in helping too, and also became a Committee member. Son, Paul, then got involved in helping with the website. As is often the way, LAA dog Toby joined the family in 2002.

Below: Toby

In singling out individuals, it is only appropriate that this chapter should end with a tribute to someone who has supported LAA for many years, and who, for the last ten years, has borne a huge burden as LAA Chair - Janet Campion. Janet was an early volunteer, back in the days of Dorothea Farndon. Joyce Kelley remembers when they first met. "I was

Above: Janet Campion, husband Bill and LAA Vice Chair Anne Martin

doing a street collection on Narborough Road, and Janet was running a hair dressing business. She asked me if I'd like some clothes and things to sell. That was the start of it. I think her mother always blamed me for roping Janet in. She would come and walk the dogs. Then she'd go and sit in the field for hours with some of the old ones. She was wonderful with those old dogs. And she was always bringing in strays. We used to say to her that she'd picked them up before they even knew they were lost! I always knew when Janet had been: the dogs were always wrapped up for the night in old woolly jumpers." Little did Janet realise when she started taking jumble down to Huncote in the early 1970s what a huge part of her life Leicester Animal Aid would become. "I certainly wouldn't have imagined what an expert I'd become about sewerage, cesspits and drainage" she admits.

Back in the early days, when there were no paid staff Janet would find herself nipping over to Huncote to clean dogs out, going off to work - as a mobile hair-dresser – and then nipping back between hair appointments to feed the dogs or put them to bed. "You can just imagine how I smelt some days" she says. With a young child she had to take a bit of a break but did manage to persuade her own mother to babysit regularly on Sundays so that she could still go and help out at LAA, helping to make sure the dogs all got a walk once a day.

It seems her talents know no bounds. Sue Stoyell first recalls meeting Janet in the bathroom of her flat – Sue was about to move in and Janet was doing all the tiling. She had already laid the carpets and hung the curtains!

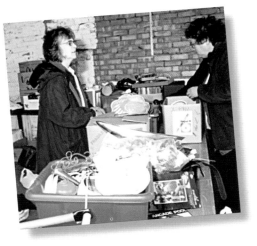

Below: Wednesday jumble sorting

Wednesday afternoon sees another side to Janet – sorting the donated goods – along with the dedicated group who assemble each week to sort whatever has been left in the shed during the previous week. No mean task this: there is apparently a real science to it: items for the shop, the Christmas Bazaar, the mini-markets, the Auction, bedding for the animals. Whatever it is, there is always a place for it.

As chair of the Management Committee for almost ten years now, Janet has overseen the biggest period of expansion LAA has ever known. Her role in chairing every site meeting, at a time when new buildings are springing up all over the site, has been immense. "But then" as she says "becoming an expert in sewerage might just come in useful one day!" Pat Bass remembers when she was Secretary, asking Janet if she would stand for Committee. Janet was doubtful as she wasn't sure she had the necessary skills. Time was certainly to prove her wrong on that score.

"Whilst a few of us on the Committee started the ball rolling" recalls Pat, "it has been Janet who has brought the plans we made to fruition. Our aim was to build a first class sanctuary with animals receiving the very best of care and it has happened. Without Janet's leadership and incredibly hard work over such a long period those plans and dreams may well have come to nothing."

In acknowledging all that Janet has done over the years for LAA, we cannot ignore the support and contribution of her husband, Bill. As the phone rings constantly late into the evening with one LAA query or another, Bill is in no doubt of his role - "the unofficial and unpaid LAA answering service!" As he says, "when Janet said it's a case of love me, love my dog, I didn't quite realise she meant all this lot!"

Above: Janet Campion with Cindy Lou

Left: Dog walker

Just before she retired Sue Stoyell summed up just how important are the volunteers: "I often reflect as to what and to whom we owe LAA's survival and success, and have come to realise how fortunate we are to have so many dedicated people involved in playing such diverse roles - the roles that are so necessary to the running of the organisation. There are the volunteers who walk the dogs, check the homes, those that help in the kennels, others who help with site maintenance and gardening, man reception, organise the shop and those who are willing to stand on committee to help manage the business decisions of the charity. The leaflets and posters are all the product of volunteers. LAA is a hive of activity. Then there are the people who make regular donations and covenants, remember LAA in their wills, keep collection boxes, collect from food bins in supermarkets, donate items for the shop and help at events. These are the unsung heroes who help to keep our gates open."

CANINE COMPANIONS:
MAN'S BEST FRIEND

Dogs are well known for their devotion to man.
They are wonderfully loyal and affectionate
companions. They deserve a second chance.
For thousands of dogs over the last fifty years,
Leicester Animal Aid has provided just that.

Top left: Dog walker with Greyhound

Right: Beauty – first LAA dog to emigrate to Australia

Above: Spike and Beccy with Milo

Over the years there have been many remarkable stories – happy and sad. To all of us who have been fortunate enough to be adopted by a Leicester Animal Aid dog – don't ever think you choose them! – we not only gain wonderful companions, but also become part of the 'family' that is LAA. Others who have passed through the gates of LAA have gone on to be wonderful 'service dogs' in one role or another – a fulfilling life suited to their personalities and temperaments and, in many cases, helping to transform the lives of their owners.

Spike had been at LAA because his first owner couldn't look after him and, although he was rehomed, he was returned because he is a bit of a 'one-person dog' and gets over-excited among a lot of people. Anabel McDougall had been looking for a small dog for some time. A friend suggested she should try LAA. When she rang, she was told about Spike, who was looking for a home with a single lady owner. Anabel recalls their first meeting. "It was February 2003, and the dogs were wearing coats against the chill. I couldn't stop thinking about him on the cold days that followed, so I decided to meet him properly. He was brought to the office but wasn't really very interested in me until I brought out the treats! Because he bonds with one person very closely, he was more interested in the staff and volunteers with whom he was more familiar. I thought he deserved a proper home and decided to adopt him. When I went to collect him, he bounded into the office and greeted me like a long lost friend, jumped into the car without a second thought and we've never looked back. Spike has proved to be an exceptional companion, good with other dogs and people, though he does have some typical 'terrier' traits". Not only did Anabel get a dog, but she subsequently found herself co-opted onto the Committee as Secretary. "So I got rather more than I bargained for when I contacted LAA, but I wouldn't have it any other way!"

Beccy Garner also took on a dog from LAA and then found herself on the Committee. Milo had come into LAA aged about 7-8 months from a family with several children. There was illness in the family and the dog had to go. It was Christmas 2001 and Beccy was delivering a food parcel from her workplace. She asked if she could look round. Milo was curled up in the front of his cage. "He looked up, gave a little wag, then tucked his head back into his body as if to say 'I know you won't be interested in me'. He absolutely had me by the heartstrings then and I went back two days later and reserved him! He had been there for three months. It was then a few weeks before I could take him home as he had to have his 'op' and then he got kennel cough. So every weekend I would go and sit in his kennel with him, fuss him and give him lots of treats. I remember the first time I took him for a walk, with my sister and her dalmation, Molly. We went to Burbage Common and Milo hadn't a clue what to do. He literally followed Molly everywhere she went." Beccy and Milo started doing agility by accident. Last year was his first year of competition and he won an armful of rosettes and a trophy. In 2005 they went to Crufts to take part in the Rescue Dog Agility Team demos (with Wood Green Animal Shelters). "How proud to be able to say you've taken your dog to Crufts. He was as good as gold, bless him."

Cindy, a German Shepherd, came into LAA one Sunday early in 2000 at midnight – hence her name. She was starved and painfully thin with nails half an inch long. She was only about four years old but looked like a really old dog. Her skin was red raw and she had scarcely any hair on her back due to a severe flea allergy. She was brought in by a lorry driver who found her in a country lane on that bleak winter night in January. Just four weeks on, she was strong enough to have a good run in the paddocks, her eyes were bright and she was clearly enjoying life. Her coat was improving as was her weight. Despite all she had been through, she had become a content and happy dog. After such a sad case, it is always nice to hear of happy endings. Cindy's new 'mum' wrote: "I thank you for allowing me to have Cindy. I couldn't wish for a better dog temperament-wise. She is wonderful with my 3 year old daughter, never growling despite being pushed to the limits and she is very protective of her. I still have problems with Cindy not liking other dogs but she loves my mum's dog. It is lovely to see the two dogs play together and Cindy will now run after the ball. She was definitely worth the wait."

Greyhound, Max, became a real ambassador for LAA, working with his 'new mum', volunteer Jan Smith. Jan already had two dogs, Flynn a black lurcher and Dusty, a black standard poodle. When Dusty was diagnosed with a brain tumour, Jan and her husband decided to look for another dog before they lost Dusty as they didn't want Flynn to be an only dog.

So, off Jan went to Animal Aid, looking for a black bitch. She met various dogs but none were suitable. Sue Stoyell then approached Jan about a dog which was desperately in need of a home. This turned out to be a white, male greyhound! At first sight Jan didn't particularly like him, but Sue persuaded her to think again. He had been brought to Animal Aid in April 1994 when one of the LAA dog walkers had been in a pub and seen someone trying to give the dog away to anyone who would take him. Maxi weighed approximately 20 kilos, barely two-thirds of his ideal

Above:: Newspaper article, Trevor Williams with Cindy and Cindy in garden with friend Meg

Below: Max with Rhona Millsom and Sparky doing a talk about LAA and Jan Smith and Max modelling at a Fashion Show in aid of LAA

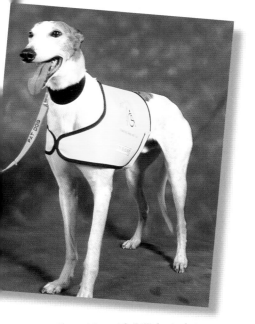

Above: Max with PAT dog jacket

weight and was very depressed. (So worried was Sue about Maxi, she would regularly spend her evenings sitting in his kennel with him).

Jan picks up the story. "I agreed to introduce him to Flynn and Dusty. Dusty looked at him and wandered off to do her own thing and Flynn bared his teeth – whoops! Then the obvious struck us. Maxi was a full dog and Flynn was neutered. Problem solved – get Maxi neutered. Job done and Flynn happily accepted him.

"Ron and I took Maxi home in August to our completely refurbished home – new carpets, curtains, redecoration etc. Maxi had problems. He had no control over his bowels or bladder – that meant carpets and curtains cleaned three times in six months. During his first week with us he cost us over £100 in vet bills just to prove there were no parasites in his gut and that there was no other problem. Everything we fed him went through undigested. He was losing more and more weight and we were desperately worried about him.

"One day in October I ran into an old friend who had his own stable of racing greyhounds. When I told him about the problem of Maxi's diet, his reply was 'Oh, we can cure that, just give him 4 Weetabix with a pint of full cream milk and sugar for breakfast followed by Wafcol soaked in water overnight in small meals throughout the day, and feed him as much as he should have if he was his proper weight.' My comment was that he already had the trots and so much milk would probably make it worse. 'Trust me' said my friend and I'm glad I did. Two weeks later Maxi had gained a stone in weight and never looked back.

Below: Max and Jan with Di, a volunteer at local hospice

"Maxi developed a lovely gentle personality – described by some as so laid back as to be virtually horizontal! The first time he wagged his tail I cried and the first time he barked, he frightened himself! He underwent assessment for Pets as Therapy and became the resident PAT Dog at local hospice, LOROS, for five years. He represented PAT dogs many times at Crufts as well as various other events around the country.

"He was always happy to help Animal Aid and to support them in any way he could, whether taking part in collections or giving talks on their behalf to raise awareness in the community.

"In April 2004, Maxi developed a limp on his front leg, which turned out to be a very aggressive form of bone cancer. So, with great sadness and many tears we had to say goodbye to our very much loved friend of nine years. Maxi asked nothing of us, but gave us everything unconditionally. Without him our lives would have been so much poorer."

Looking at Benji now it is hard to believe he hasn't always had a wonderful life. He is a dog so full of fun and with the kind of face that seems to be permanently laughing. He was brought into LAA one Christmas a few years ago, having been ill-treated and was very poorly. He spent Christmas in Sue Stoyell's flat, even undergoing an operation on Christmas Day. For 'new mum' Rosemary Hall, Benji was just the right dog. Benji has proved a 'real gem', going on to gain his Silver Good Citizen Award, become a PAT dog and a regular visitor to an old people's home, as well as excelling at agility.

A number of dogs from Huncote dogs have found a good home in the armed services.

Danny, a very active border collie, with huge ears, who came into the kennels in 1995, needed a home that could cope with all his surplus energy. He found just that. He showed real potential in the kennels with his great enjoyment of ball games, especially when he had to find the ball in long grass. With all his energy it was clear he would be much happier as a working dog rather than as a pet, so HM Forces took him on a trial basis. He passed his exams with flying colours and took on the role of a sniffer dog.

Jess, a short haired German pointer came into Huncote early in 1997, aged just 15 months. She was an extremely active dog, and had been difficult to control in a home environment. The Forces Assessor was convinced she was a natural "sniffer" dog and was happy to take her on for training. She went on to be a very successful dog for Customs and Excise, working for them at docks around the country.

Jock, a Labrador from LAA joined the army, and underwent the usual rigorous fitness and intelligence tests before being accepted. After passing these with flying colours, he went on to serve in Europe with his handler, who reported that "Jock was the best dog he has ever had to train." No small accolade for a previously unwanted dog that found himself a happy and active new home.

Above: Rosemary Hall and Benji

Below: Customs and Excise letter about Jess and postcard of Customs and Excise dogs, Jess second from left, top

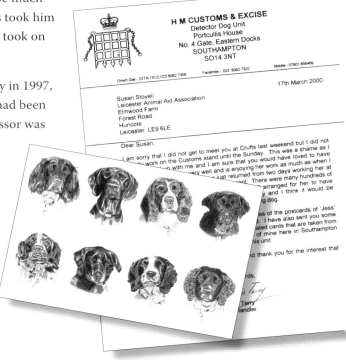

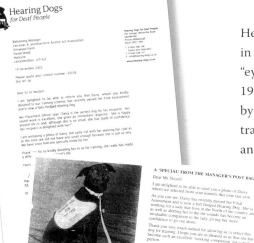

Above: Letter from Hearing Dogs and a Newsletter article about Daisy, one of the first LAA dogs to become a Hearing Dog

Hearing Dogs for the Deaf train dogs to act as "ears" for deaf people, in much the same way as Guide Dogs for the Blind train dogs to be the "eyes" of blind people. They use mainly rescue dogs and in the autumn 1995 Bess, a little black and white mongrel was taken on trial from LAA by Hearing Dogs – the first dog from Huncote to be selected for the training programme. Bess successfully completed her socialisation period and went on to qualify for the intensive training needed for hearing dogs.

Bess was followed by many other dogs, including: Susie a Yorkie, Daisy a black mongrel and Hannah. Daisy passed her final assessment to become a fully fledged Hearing Dog. She went on to work for a lady living in the north of England and "as well as alerting her to sounds, became an invaluable companion, giving her owner the confidence to go out alone."

Another dog to make the grade as a hearing dog was Bingo. Bingo first came to Huncote as a puppy in 1998. He was obviously highly intelligent and very trainable, and was quickly spotted by kennel staff who thought he would be suitable for training as a Hearing Dog. He also successfully completed his training and became an excellent working companion.

'Bravery award for pint sized hero' and 'Daisy saves the day' were just some of the headlines for Daisy, a former LAA resident and Hearing Dog for the Deaf. Daisy has the claim to fame of being the smallest dog that Hearing Dogs for the Deaf has ever had – weighing in at just 1.6 kg. But the tiny Yorkshire Terrier very quickly showed that what she lacked in size, she more than made up for in courage, intelligence and personality, having alerted her new owner, Vonnie Truscott, of a fire danger at her home. The little dog ended up with a bravery award from the firefighters who came out to answer the fire alarm. Luckily on that occasion there was no fire but, if there had been one, Daisy would undoubtedly have saved her owner's life.

Daisy saves the day by lying down on the job in Vonnie's kitchen

FIRE ALARM PUTS PINT-SIZED HERO ON ALL-ACTION ALERT

Daisy was taken on by Hearing Dogs for the Deaf when she was just four months old. Around 74% of all Hearing Dogs were once rescued or unwanted. They spend time with socialisers before going through 16 weeks

● TOP DOG: Daisy pictured in a fireman's helmet with owner Vonnie Truscott

Daisy proves she's a livesaver

of sound-work training. This involves someone from Hearing Dogs spending time in the prospective owner's house and recording all the different sounds so that the dog can be trained to react to each of them. Hearing Dogs alert deaf people by touch, using a paw, or jumping up and down and leading the person back to the sound source. They lay down to indicate danger. It was December 2002 when a letter from Hearing Dogs was received at LAA saying that Daisy had recently passed her final assessment to become a fully fledged Hearing Dog. Her placement officer commented: "Daisy is the perfect dog for the recipient. Her sound work is excellent, she gives an immediate response. She is happy around shops and although she is so small she has loads of confidence. Her recipient is delighted with her." The challenge was in having a specially made coat for Daisy as she was so tiny none of the standard sizes fitted!

It must be unusual to have three dogs from one family all becoming Hearing Dogs for the Deaf but that is what happened to Poodles, Angel and puppies, Holly and Robin. Theirs really was a rescue story with a happy ending. It was Christmas 2000 when a local postwoman actually saw the three dogs being thrown out of a van onto the road before the owner sped off. She managed to catch two of them and the next day found the third. All three were taken into LAA, where they were given their new seasonal names. They would never have survived out in the cold but thanks to the dedication of LAA staff who cared for them – they all had long nails and matted coats – they thrived and were put forward for training as Hearing Dogs. All three passed and eventually went their separate ways – Angel to Devon, Robin to Scotland and Holly to London.

Probably not many people know that dogs sometimes need blood transfusions, and can act as blood donors, just as humans do. In August 2003, LAA Greyhound Ben hit the headlines in a big way. 'Hail the doggy donor'. 'Hero Ben is more bloodhound than greyhound.' Ben had become a regular blood donor and had been responsible for helping a number of other dogs which had needed blood transfusions. Greyhounds are particularly good for giving blood because they are calm, big and make blood up again quickly. The dogs on the donor register are on emergency standby which means there might be a call in the middle of the night. These can be life and death situations. It is one dog saving the life of another. Dogs sick with tumours, internal bleeding or needing an operation often need blood. Vets take 300ml – about the size of a can of Coke – from the dog donor through a vein in the neck, while a drip replaces the lost blood with fluids. Gentle dogs are quite

HEARING DOGS OF THE MONTH – DECEMBER 2001

Names: **HOLLY, ROBIN & ANGEL**   Breed: **POODLE**

CHRISTMAS CRACKERS

RESCUE: ABANDONED POODLES HAVE BEEN TRAINED TO HELP THE DEAF

A happy end to shaggy dog tale

Top: Hearing Dogs for the Deaf Poster: Poodles, Robin, Angel and Holly

Right: Robin

Below: Ben in the News

GIVING BLOOD: GREYHOUND BEN HELPS HIS CANINE FRIENDS

It's a dog's life-saver

Top left: Sue Stoyell and Ben

Right: Ben and Mollie

Below: Sparky article and at home in the snow and with Seth

Sparky goes from stray to TV star

And his plight touches the hearts of film crew

by Claire Jones

happy while they are donating blood, others may need some sedation. The sick dog receives the blood through a vein in the leg. Before the dog donor blood register, vets had to rely on donations from their own pets and those of colleagues. It was a moving occasion when Ben met two year old grey mongrel, Mollie, for the first time since his donated blood brought her back from the brink of death during an operation. They met at a blood doning session – for humans. Hero, Ben, was presented with a certificate from the National Blood Transfusion Service for his lifesaving doggy donations. Not long afterwards Ben was successfully rehomed.

Perhaps one of the best known LAA dogs is Sparky. It is also one of the happiest endings and a tribute to all at LAA who went to such lengths to ensure he received the best possible care. The cute little terrier, brought in as a stray aged about 6 months, was filmed by Channel 4's Pet Rescue crew to be featured as part of a new series starting in September 1998. The plight of Sparky, who was suspected of having a muscle wasting disease akin to the human condition of cerebral palsy, moved crew members so much they decided to raise funds for his treatment. Several of the crew took part in a sponsored swim for Sparky to help raise funds for tests to be carried out at the Animal Health Trust in Newmarket. It turned out that he had an incurable brain condition. Sparky's condition meant that he had serious coordination problems which made him wobble when he walked and stopped him running. Tomlinsons Boarding Kennels and Canine Hotel at Markfield came to his aid with special physiotherapy – use of its deluxe doggy swimming pool. It was considered unlikely that Sparky's coordination problems would get any worse and that meant he could be homed without particular worries about a new owner facing expensive vet bills, and in fact the vet bills would be covered by LAA under the foster dog scheme. Tomlinson's deputy manager, Claire Read, had been supervising Sparky's swimming and wanted him straight away.

Two years on, Sparky had lost his sight. Supporters at LAA pledged to raise the £1,000 necessary for an operation that would restore the sight of one eye. Since the eye operation his quality of life improved tremendously and he certainly gained in confidence. Sadly it was not possible to operate on the other eye.

Sparky took to family life like a duck to water, managing amazingly well despite his problems, and sharing in the excitement of a new addition in the family – baby Seth, even contributing regular articles for the Newsletter. "Its not taken long for Seth to find his feet and boy does he move around now. I follow him everywhere but he takes some keeping up with. Don lets me sit on top of the pushchair where I can see what's going on without tiring myself out. Family life is great, and I'm really enjoying myself – and I still get to have my regular swimming sessions. Just perfect!"

For 'mum' Claire, Sparky is certainly a very special little dog and a real character. "Sparky just loves Christmas and opens all his own presents. We can't leave them under the tree because he just opens them. Considering everything, he settles into new environments really easily. We often go on camping/walking holidays. Sparky loves these, travelling in his own purpose designed carrier. Claire and Don adapted a backpack from trial and error methods of carrying Sparky when he became tired or was unable to manage rough terrain. One major drawback of the backpack was the number of comments from the public who thought we were being cruel, ridiculous and making him lazy. We cured this by writing 'I'm not lazy I'm disabled' and the comments stopped! Sparks got 100% more attention, people got to know him by name, and he just laps it up! It seems his talents know no bounds. He sings to the harmonica and is fantastic with children – useful as Claire worked as a childminder for two years. I could go on and on but basically he is a very special little dog. He has the spirit to deal with his problems and he loves life. We're very lucky to live with him."

Top: Sparky with owner, Claire

Some of the tales will fill with horror: the dog abandoned by its owner in a field, told to stay, and then left; the dogs tied to, or thrown over the gates of LAA; the dog given away in a pub, or thrown down a well; the old dog with just days to live abandoned on the street; or the little puppy with its tail hacked off. Not all the dogs survived. In telling the stories of some, we remember them all. Thanks to the dedicated care of staff and volunteers at LAA, for many dogs, despite such dreadful starts in life, there were happy endings – the gift of a second chance.

Trevor Williams with Sanctuary dogs, Dennis and Billy

CATS, RABBITS AND THE REST:

9 LIVES AT LEAST

From the very early days Dorothea Farndon ran a cat rescue operation from her back garden, but it was only really in the mid 1990s that cats first started to be taken in at Huncote.

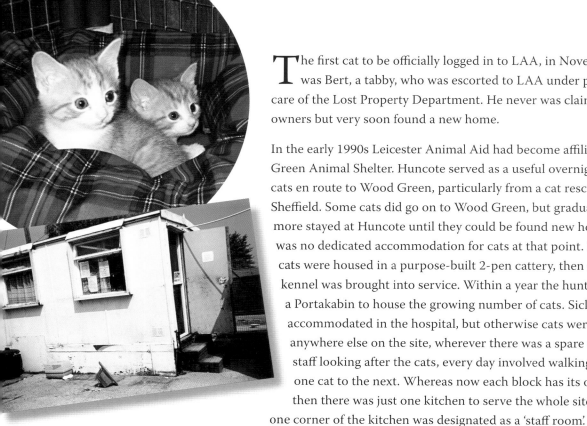

Above: Two rescued kittens and the old cattery portakabin

Below: 'Slopping out' time

The first cat to be officially logged in to LAA, in November 1995, was Bert, a tabby, who was escorted to LAA under police escort care of the Lost Property Department. He never was claimed by his owners but very soon found a new home.

In the early 1990s Leicester Animal Aid had become affiliated to Wood Green Animal Shelter. Huncote served as a useful overnight stop for cats en route to Wood Green, particularly from a cat rescue centre in Sheffield. Some cats did go on to Wood Green, but gradually more and more stayed at Huncote until they could be found new homes. There was no dedicated accommodation for cats at that point. Initially the cats were housed in a purpose-built 2-pen cattery, then an old dog kennel was brought into service. Within a year the hunt was on for a Portakabin to house the growing number of cats. Sick cats were accommodated in the hospital, but otherwise cats were housed anywhere else on the site, wherever there was a spare corner. For staff looking after the cats, every day involved walking miles from one cat to the next. Whereas now each block has its own kitchen, then there was just one kitchen to serve the whole site and even then one corner of the kitchen was designated as a 'staff room'.

Accommodating litters of kittens was a major challenge. More often than not the bathroom of Sue Stoyell's flat would be brought into use. Finding space for three litters (a total of eleven kittens) at one time was probably pushing things to the absolute limit: one litter occupied the lounge, the second the bedroom, and the third took over the bathroom. One litter had been born to a feral mother, another survived when their mother was killed in a car accident. Caring for such young kittens can be tricky: these were all aged between about two days and two weeks old when they were brought in, but all survived and were successfully rehomed – a major source of satisfaction to all those involved in caring for them, and well worth all those sleepless nights. Even though the new cattery is now in use, staff are still having their share of sleepless nights as a great many litters have been taken home and hand-reared.

The log of cats taken into Huncote makes fascinating and, at the same time, distressing, reading. There is a long catalogue of the usual reasons: stray, cats unwanted and abandoned by owners, cats left behind when owners were evicted, domestic problems, fleas, and danger of busy roads. Allergies in the family, particularly in young children, is a fairly common reason why a family might have to hand a cat in for rehoming. Often a cat would produce an unwanted litter. One kitten was handed in for rehoming because "it kept behaving like a kitten!" Cats and kittens were found in cardboard boxes, dumped under hedges and, on one occasion, found tied up in a plastic bag in the gateway at LAA. Sometimes cats were handed in or abandoned because it was too much trouble to groom them, and their coats had become completely unmanageable. One long-haired cat was unable to lie down in comfort, so matted was its coat. Shorn of all the tangles, it looked a sorry sight but was certainly much happier and more comfortable. One entry in the log conjures up a wonderful picture: the cat had to go because it kept tripping up an elderly uncle!

Already by 1996, despite the limited facilities, over 50 adult cats and 60 kittens had been homed.

It soon became clear that unwanted cats needed just as much help as the dogs. In order to reduce the growing number of unwanted cats and kittens, there was also an urgent need to pursue a neutering policy, for domestic cats and the ever increasing feral cat population.

Above: Sue Stoyell at LAA stand at the Cat Show, NEC

Below: Rescued cats

The problem of unneutered feral cats remains a significant one. Adult feral cats cannot be rehomed: the advice for anyone coming across one is to leave it where it is, but make sure there is food and water. It is also vital that shelter is provided: this led to LAA commissioning some simple feral cat shelters which are on sale and provide a small but useful income. In late 2003 LAA faced its greatest challenge in respect of feral cats when an unusual SOS message was received. A nearby industrial estate was overrun with feral cats. This was clearly going to be a major operation, and the help of several other cat rescue organisations was needed. Over several days many of the cats and kittens were caught – a total of 30 in all. Rehoming the kittens, once they had been socialised, was a very real possibility. For the adult cats, who were used to living outside, this would not have been realistic. For them, neutering to ensure that no more unwanted litters were born, and then release back to home territory was the answer.

Once cats began to be taken in officially at Huncote, it wasn't too long before they really began to find their feet. The Spons-a-Dog scheme had been in operation for some time when Gizmo became the first Spons-a-Cat. No sense of modesty with Gizmo. In her own words, she was "a beautiful black 8 year old cat, who had done it at last, by invading the canine bastion!"

Above: Foundations of the new cattery and John Rogers (builder) outside the new cattery

Below: Visitors looking at a cat in it's 'sitting room'

The first cat to benefit from the foster scheme was Gandalf. He was found one Sunday afternoon lying in the middle of the road. When taken home by a passer by he started to have fits and so LAA were called to come and collect him. He was very underweight and diagnosed as having chronic kidney disease. Julie Rulton, then head of cats at LAA, took him home where he spent his remaining few months in a happy home environment, including sneaking to the neighbours and stealing their cats' food.

One real feline character, remembered with affection by staff was Marlene. She was a large ginger cat, who had been seen on site several times one summer. One afternoon she led staff to a litter of four kittens and then promptly vanished, obviously convinced that the kittens would be well looked after – not the usual form of abandonment! The kittens thrived. Eventually, after a lot of patience and some tasty titbits, Marlene the mum was caught. All were eventually rehomed.

While new kennel blocks were rapidly being built, there was mounting pressure to build a suitable home for the growing number of feline residents. The opening of the new purpose-designed Cattery in February 2002 was a dream come true, for the cats and the staff and volunteers who looked after them. As with all aspects of LAA life, a real tribute must be paid to the dedicated band of cat volunteers, feeding, cleaning out, and generally helping with the cats. The staff would be lost, and certainly wouldn't cope, without them. Eighteen months in the planning and very much longer in the dreaming, the new cattery was completed at a cost of over £100,000. The money, raised from grants and legacies, meant an end to the old makeshift accommodation, and provided space for 30 cats in comfortable, purpose-built pens, with sleeping and exercise areas. The Cattery also included an isolation area and a nursery. The food preparation area is within the cattery block, so cats can watch their food being prepared. For visitors there is the chance to view the cats in their own 'sitting rooms', each one individually furnished with a bed, knitted or crocheted blanket, and selection of toys. Classical music adds to the ambience. One new owner, on arriving to collect her cat, proudly announced that she had the car radio tuned to Classic FM as she knew that's what the cats were used to!

There was much debate as to who should be invited to formally open the new Cattery. An obvious, and very appropriate, local solution was found, and the Cattery was formally opened at Family Fun Day. The local Huncote amateur dramatic society (HATS) was in the middle of rehearsals for a production of Dick Whittington. So the task of cutting the ribbon and declaring the Cattery open was performed by Dick himself, with trusty cat in supporting role!

The LAA record for the cat being rehomed the most number of times goes to Heskey, who is now in his fifth and, hopefully, final home. He originally arrived at LAA in a box left at the gate with his mother and two siblings. He was then just 3 months old. He was homed with his brother but they were soon returned for scratching the wallpaper. They were found a new home together but unfortunately this was also short-lived due to one or both of them messing in the house. Luckily another home was found where they stayed for some time. Sadly though Heskey's brother was killed in a road accident. Heskey again ended up at the Cattery when his owner was moving and unable to take him. His fourth home was with a family who also had several other pets and, although they persevered for a while, it became obvious that he wasn't happy – so back he came again! Poor Heskey was now about 5 years old and very unsettled, still looking for the perfect home. His chance finally arrived one Sunday when Andy and Claire fell in love with him despite his history and took him home. That is almost the end of his story – except for escaping the afternoon he went to his new home, and being found a week later on a roof, several ongoing health problems and occasional house-training mistakes. Heskey reckons he now has his paws very firmly under the table and doesn't intend moving anywhere again!

Another memorable cat rescue was Cracker. A phone call was received from a local school just before Christmas. It was the day of their Christmas dinner and a 'large pregnant cat' had arrived on the doorstep expecting to join in the festivities. When Sue and Julie went to collect the cat they found that, despite being very large, it was in fact a male. He appeared to be having some breathing difficulties, which is probably why it was assumed he was pregnant. After being rushed to the vet, he was diagnosed as having a heart problem. He was put on medication, with a warning that he might only live for about 6 months. Karen, one of the LAA volunteer dog walkers, heard his story and decided to take him home. Six months came and went and Cracker is still going strong, very happy in his new home.

Within just a year or two of opening the Cattery is constantly full, with a waiting list in operation. The cat sanctuary has four long-stay residents. Already there is talk of an extension! Custer, a large black and white cat, arrived as a stray in October 1999. He was found to have

Above: Huncote amateur dramatic society at the Cattery opening and the Cattery storage

Below: Visitor viewing cats and Cracker

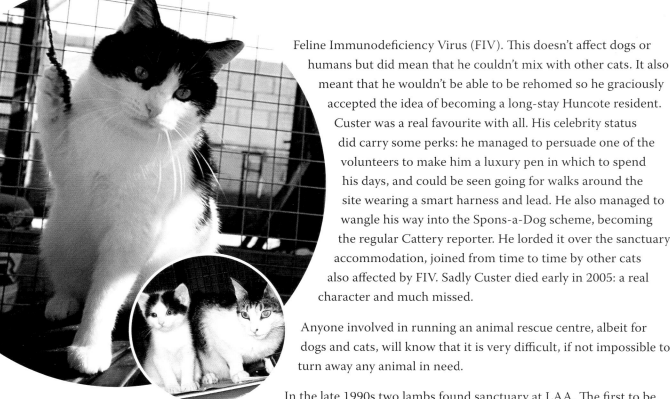

Feline Immunodeficiency Virus (FIV). This doesn't affect dogs or humans but did mean that he couldn't mix with other cats. It also meant that he wouldn't be able to be rehomed so he graciously accepted the idea of becoming a long-stay Huncote resident. Custer was a real favourite with all. His celebrity status did carry some perks: he managed to persuade one of the volunteers to make him a luxury pen in which to spend his days, and could be seen going for walks around the site wearing a smart harness and lead. He also managed to wangle his way into the Spons-a-Dog scheme, becoming the regular Cattery reporter. He lorded it over the sanctuary accommodation, joined from time to time by other cats also affected by FIV. Sadly Custer died early in 2005: a real character and much missed.

Anyone involved in running an animal rescue centre, albeit for dogs and cats, will know that it is very difficult, if not impossible to turn away any animal in need.

In the late 1990s two lambs found sanctuary at LAA. The first to be taken in, in the summer of 1996, was a beautiful little black lamb, with a dense wiry coat, hence the nickname of 'Brillo'. The tiny lamb had been born at the side of a fence, close to a steep bank. She had stumbled through the fence and fallen down the bank, becoming separated from her mother. When she arrived at the kennels she was quite weak, and very cold. Her chances of survival looked slim. However, with constant two-hourly feeds and lots of warmth, she quickly gained weight and strength. Joining the menagerie of a hen, rooster and several rabbits who were in situ at the kennels at that time, Brillo very quickly started to enjoy herself despite her inauspicious start to life.

In the spring of 1999, the second lamb, Freeway, was taken in. Freeway was so named because he was found stranded on the central reservation of the M1 motorway. The terrified animal was picked up by police and given overnight sanctuary by a nearby farmer. When it was time to move on, LAA again offered sanctuary. He was only about three or four weeks old at that point, and needed bottle feeding. Kennel maid, Jodie Barlow, hand-reared Freeway and cared for him until he went to live with Val Earp, Assistant Kennel Manager, who already had sheep.

Top: Custer

Right: Two rescued cats

Below: Brillo

Bottom: Freeway and Jodie Barlow

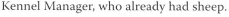

And then there were the rabbits!

One of the sadder events of the 1994 Christmas Bazaar was the discovery of two small brown and white rabbits left at the gates of LAA. They were huddled in a small cardboard box with RABBITS UNWANTED written across the top. They were luckily none the worse for their ordeal and were subsequently homed with a member of staff who had a great deal of experience in caring for rabbits.

Later a small pet area was planned. Unfortunately some of the first rabbits to be taken in were pregnant. Staff at the time recall: "There were rabbits everywhere. Every rabbit had to be checked out by a vet. We could only ask for a donation of £5 for each rabbit and it was costing us more than that for the vet's bills. At our peak we were trying to cope with 52 rabbits. It just wasn't viable in terms of space or funding, and the Committee took the decision that we could no longer take in rabbits. Instead we now work with a rabbit rescue centre, which is fortunately able to accept all our referrals."

Given all the pressures over the years, probably the last thing that was needed were a pair of donkeys. But Mrs Farndon was convinced that they had to have donkeys. "She bought one, and then she bought the other" recalls Joyce Kelley. "Jubilee and Pippin they were called, and they weren't even waifs and strays in need of a home. Freebie, the Pyrrenean Mountain Dog loved them, and you'd often find him in their field." They were real characters, though not easy to handle, particularly when they knew that the farrier was on his way. They would also chase the dog walkers whenever they ventured into their field. Eventually some members of the Committee decided that the donkeys had to go. Mrs Farndon had died by then. The Donkey Sanctuary in Devon was contacted. It was a sad day when Jubilee and Pippin departed, but ironically they eventually found a wonderful home just forty miles from Huncote!

Bottom and below: Jubilee and Pippin

THE
N E X T
PEN
IS PEN IS SPONSORED
N E X T plc

REACHING OUT:
LAA AND THE COMMUNITY

An organisation like Leicester Animal Aid does not exist in isolation, but is very much at the heart of the local community. Over the years a wide range of links have been fostered in a variety of ways.

Above: LAA Front Gates, Huncote

Below: RAF Cottesmore – Dog handler at Open Day 2003 and presenting Sue Stoyell with a cheque

For the last thirty five years Leicester Animal Aid has been based at Huncote. During that time LAA has become firmly embedded in the local community, to the benefit of both. For a start many of the volunteers are drawn from the local area, many local people have taken on LAA dogs or cats, many are loyal supporters of fund raising or other events. Opening the doors and spreading the word about the work of LAA, and encouraging responsible pet ownership, can only be of benefit in helping to reduce the number of unwanted pets.

The last few years have seen real progress in development of links with the local community, something that Sue Stoyell was always very keen to promote. This has involved staff and volunteers of LAA going out and giving talks about the work of LAA, features in local newsletters, regular radio slots and stands at local events, but also encouraging individuals, groups and organisations to visit the Huncote site to get to know more about, and possibly get involved with, the work of this remarkable organisation. The range of organisations, and the type of involvement, is very varied, from visits by local brownie packs to large corporate organisations and the RAF. It is the continuing links with some of these organisations that is a testament to all that LAA stands for.

Members of RAF Cottesmore Dog Section have been supportive friends of LAA for many years. They have thrown their weight behind fundraising campaigns, including raising money from boarding dogs from the camp and donating the proceeds, thereby enabling LAA to purchase a large shed for one of the dogs' play areas, named aptly Cottesmore Cottage. Other donations have included a grooming table and weighing machine, and seemingly endless supplies of blankets, delivered by the van load. Practical help on site is always welcome and on more than one occasion their muscle power has come into its own with help dismantling portakabins and painting blocks. A dog handling display at Open Day 2003 proved a great attraction with the crowds.

Practical help on site has also been provided by Community Service. Over the years many site projects, both in teams and by individuals, have been undertaken. Projects have been mostly related to site management, but more recently have included improvements to the Cat Sanctuary pen, where some of the long stay residents spend their days. Products, such as hedgehog boxes, cat shelters and garden furniture from the Community Service workshops, are regularly brought in for sale on site at LAA.

For many years Leicester Animal Aid has offered placements to Brooksby College students taking NVQs and National Diplomas in Animal Care.

More recently Brooksby students have undertaken a number of projects such as creating a play area for the Sanctuary dogs and are now very involved in creating and maintaining the conservation areas on the site. Instructor, Cherolyn Huff, is a regular guest speaker at Huncote Hound Club meetings, bringing along some of the more unusual Brooksby residents, as well as contributing regular articles on careers with animals to the LAA Newsletter. Local schools and colleges also take advantage of opportunities for work experience placements for their students.

Links with local company, Next plc, have continued to prosper over the years. Since making a Millenium donation in 1999, Next has continued to support LAA with regular donations ever since, including sponsoring a pen. There are always regular Christmas donations of food and toys for the animals. Staff of Next have baked countless cakes for sale at Open Days and Family Fun Days, weathering many a soggy event cheerfully and always profitably. More recently they have provided the fittings for the new shop in the Visitor/Education Centre.

LAA has also become increasingly involved in village life. Talks on the work of LAA are regularly given to local schools and groups. Some five years ago, Father Nick Burton of St James the Greater Church in Huncote took up the suggestion of holding an annual service for village pets and LAA animals. The pet blessing service, which attracts a wide range of animals, has proved immensely popular, and gives a real focus to the importance of pets in homes and their place in our society.

Above: Cherolyn Huff – Huncote Hound Club, a Conservation area and Jodie Barlow in the Next pen

Below: Pet Blessing Service

In 1996 LAA took over responsibility for Petfinder, the service which re-unites lost pets with their owners. The service which had a very high success rate in re-uniting pets with their owners was under threat of closure as the previous operators were unable to continue with the service. "Co-ordinating Petfinder was both a rewarding experience and occasionally nerve-racking and frustrating" according to Ann Amos. "Frustrating because there should be no need for the service at all if owners of animals made sure that their pets were identifiable. But it's always rewarding when we manage to reunite a lost pet with its owner. Over the years there have been many happy endings. It isn't only cats and dogs who get themselves lost. Some years ago a barn owl reported himself lost by landing on the roof of a local Police Station. The police rang Petfinder to report him found! Luckily the owner rang not long afterwards and the two were re-united."

Vicky Arscott became involved in coordinating Petfinder while working at Radio Leicester, which supported Petfinder by featuring regular

Above: Petfinder leaflet and Vicky Arscott's dog, Luke

bulletins on lost and found pets. Every day she would go home from work to a Petfinder line that would ring constantly. A real animal lover herself, Vicky could sympathise with those who had lost a pet. Though she never met any of the owners, it was always a great relief when the owners rang to let her know their pet had been found. One or two favourites had particularly happy endings. An elderly man was out walking his equally elderly, and blind, dog – a Golden Retriever. On the walk the man became ill and fell. The dog wandered away and lost its bearings. The man was unhurt and taken home but desperately distressed about his missing dog. The dog was found in a nearby corn field, equally distressed and disoriented. The man's neighbours, anxious to avoid a repeat of such a worrying time, insisted in future that the man let someone know when he was going out and when he got back. Perhaps one of the strangest missing pets was Henry, the tortoise. Henry lived in a first floor flat but one day got out, trotted off and became lost. Alerted by posters displayed locally, neighbours scoured the area. Ten days after his escape bid, Henry was spotted a mile and a half away happily munching his way through somebody's vegetable patch. Henry and owner were happily reunited. It was only natural that Vicky would find herself taking on an LAA dog. Like many, despite a dreadful start in life, Luke, a German Shepherd/Greyhound X, has turned into the most wonderful pet.

In February 2001 Lesley Dawes-Gamble, a member of LAA Management Committee, took over coordination of Petfinder. One of her first successes was a little foxy X-breed who amazed everyone by waiting 13 years before making his first bid for freedom. He skipped off to a neighbouring village, sampled the wares of the local "chippy" and then moved on to the next village, spending much of his time commuting between the two. After several days all search activities were focused on the "food" village and local villagers were all caught up in the hunt for the chip loving hound. Finally, on the main road, trotting leisurely towards the chippy, dog met owner and were noisily reunited. Totally unexpected to Lesley, as Coordinator, was the spring migration of the tortoise. Not renowned for going missing, these creatures seem to awaken, stretch, amble over to the food, take a crafty look around, tiptoe to the fence then make a dash for the fields. "So far" recalled Lesley "there has been 100% recovery rate for the tortoises, despite one of them heading for the train station!" Pat Green, former Committee member, took over the task of Petfinder Coordinator in April 2005.

Over the years, LAA has maintained close links with Radio Leicester. Monica Winfield, presenter of the afternoon show, did two outside broadcasts from LAA. "They were great fun" recalls Monica. "We would turn up in the radio car, put up the mast, and then just wander round the site. We were given open access to go anywhere, and talk to anybody. What struck me instantly was the lack of glamour, the crumbling drive, the car park full of potholes, but it was so clear that the animals came first, and the enthusiasm of everyone we met, whether staff or volunteers, was infectious. And they knew so much. If the notice on the dog's pen said – "chases bikes" or "not good with small children" they could tell you so much about the dog's likes and dislikes. On one occasion we met the animal behaviourist, who talked to us about her work. It was incredible the number of phone calls we took after that broadcast. You would have thought everyone in Leicester had a problem dog. But the main message was that usually it's a question of sorting the owner before you go on to sort the dog!"

Some time later when Monica found herself in a position to take on a dog, she didn't consider going anywhere else but Huncote. Beau, an 8 year old dog, supposedly a Spaniel/Rottweiler X, though now considered more likely to be a Gordon Setter, albeit a short-legged one, proved to be the one. Not only has Beau become a great pet, but his nice nature made him an ideal candidate for training as a PAT dog, and he and Monica are now regular visitors to a local hospital.

Education and promotion of responsible pet ownership are a key role for LAA, and indeed any other rescue organisation, and so the idea of creating a club for junior members was born. Sue Stoyell had a gently persuasive manner. "Sue Ablett was a keen volunteer and member of the Marketing Committee, and seemed ideal to help launch Huncote Hound Club. Protestations that surely someone more used to children would be better were swept swiftly aside. Of course there was the additional lure of Fozzie, her 'Huncote Hound' becoming the Club's first mascot – though maybe not the best choice as he wasn't very used to children either!" The rest, as they say, is history.

Huncote Hound Club was launched officially at Family Fun Day in August 2001. The initial aims were modest – 25 members in the first year. Sue Ablett recalls: "By the time of the first Activity Day, in November 2001, we already had a good number of members. We had no idea how many members would come. Anticipating half a dozen at most, the idea of launching the Club by providing a picnic lunch seemed a good idea. The rolls and eggs were bought. And then

Above: Monica Winfield and Beau

Below: Huncote Hound Club - Sue Stoyell with Club and the First Activity Day.

Above: Huncote Hound Club: Ken Goodrich of the RSPB leading a birdwatching session and Littlethorpe Farm Sanctuary visit

Below: Official opening of the Huncote Hound Club hide, Huncote Hound Club Flier and planting in the copse.

the numbers kept going up, so that by the actual day we were expecting 20 members. More rolls had to be bought. There were egg sandwiches everywhere!" That first meeting was a tremendous success. It even resulted in a little kitten being rehomed. As mum and dad came to pick up their children at the end of the day, they were dragged straight off to see the little chap. Fortunately they fell for him too! Ever since that first meeting the Club has continued to grow and prosper, peaking at 40 members in the first year.

Over the years Club members have had talks on a wide range of topics: Hearing Dogs for the Deaf; caring for your pet (dogs, cats and rabbits); Hedgehog, Tortoise, and Rabbit and Guinea Pig Rescue organisations, and PAT dogs. Outdoor sessions have focussed on birdwatching for beginners and conservation: the Huncote site offers great opportunities for both activities, and now boasts its very own Huncote Hound Club hide. A real highlight and now an annual event is the visit to nearby Littlethorpe Farm Sanctuary where Club members have the opportunity to meet the rescued sheep, goats and horses; help clean them out and feed them, and try their riding skills. The quarterly newsletter, The Huncote Hound Club Flier, has become a popular feature full of tips on caring for animals, and with members contributing and writing about their own pets. The members themselves greatly enjoy all that the Club has to offer. As for the parents – who are, of course, excluded from all Club activities – they think it's a great idea. "That first Activity Day was wonderful" said one mum, "no children for a whole day. I can't believe just how much I got done! When's the next one?"

The Activity Days are always a great opportunity for Club members to see the new animals that have come in and hear their stories, but also to catch up on some on the long-stay animals. "Can't we touch them?" is a constant refrain. Many are frustrated that they aren't yet old enough to help out with dog walking. So, the idea of asking Club members to help out with socialising young puppies and kittens went down really well. The hope is that membership of Huncote Hound Club will lead the young members on to become volunteers when they become older: already the first Club member, Liz Dunderdale, has completed a period of work experience at LAA.

For Huncote Hound, Fozzie the role of Club mascot was just one of his many claims to fame. It does keep him fairly busy, with a regular column in the Flier, and then of course there are the occasional guest appearances. All a bit exhausting and a far cry from when he first arrived at Huncote. Fozzie has become something of an ambassador for Leicester Animal Aid. Like many of the dogs that pass through the gates of LAA, he certainly didn't have the best start in life. Picked up as a stray, aged about one, he then spent eleven months at Huncote. Despite the care and affection of staff and helpers it was just long enough to become stressed, depressed, and pretty institutionalised, or at least that's how he seemed. He has a very different story – something about just biding his time until his new 'mum' came along. From that day on he never looked back. Sure he had a few problems to overcome, but he quickly hit the headlines in a national dog magazine winning Scruff of the Month feature – just a little article he wrote; auditioned – albeit unsuccessfully – for a stage role in a local production of Annie; got his Good Citizen Award, and then became pin-up boy for Leicester Animal Aid when he agreed to his photo going on the front of the Publicity Leaflet. That was such a great photo he even agreed to a life-size cardboard cut-out being made to help draw the crowds during street collections.

It was the success of Huncote Hound Club for junior members that prompted the idea of doing something specifically for the older age group. And so it was, in the summer of 2002, that the 'T' Time Tours for the Over 60's were launched, and 'No' Fozzie isn't the mascot for that!

When the boarding block ceased to operate, Leicester Animal Aid took over the strays contract for Blaby District Council, and Oadby and Wigston Council, taking responsibility and ownership of dogs left unclaimed after the statutory seven days. That link with Blaby District Council has gone from strength to strength. In 2004, thanks to the support of Councillor Jill Blackwell, Chairman of the Council, LAA was selected as one of the Council's adopted charities, benefiting from a number of fundraising events. It was a wonderfully proud moment when, at an awards ceremony in October 2004, LAA was announced winner of the first Blaby District Council Award for Outstanding Business Contribution to the well-being of the District. That award was made in recognition of the fact that, "although primarily an animal rescue organisation, LAA also has an extremely effective and wide ranging policy of community involvement". Coming just one month before Sue Stoyell's retirement, it was a fitting tribute to all the community projects she had both initiated and been involved in. Now with the new Visitor and Education centre, there will be even greater opportunities for extending links with the local community.

Above: Fozzie on front cover of the publicity leaflet

Below: Certificate Blaby District Council Award , Award ceremony, Article from Blaby Chronicle

THE FUTURE:
FULFILLING THE DREAM

In concluding this celebration of all that has been achieved over the last fifty years of Leicester Animal Aid's history, it is fascinating to speculate on the possible content of 'Telling Tails: The Sequel', produced in 2056 to mark the Centenary of LAA.

Above: Financial Crisis leaflet, Press Cutting and Scamp and Molly – 50th Anniversary mascots

Below: Keely Short with young volunteers, fundraising at Open Day 2005

Above: Out with the old: old portakabin being moved off site

Even as we begin to look forward to the next half century, however, Leicester Animal Aid is facing a major financial crisis, and one which casts a shadow over the celebrations and threatens the very future of the Centre. This is not a new situation. Over the years there have been other crises. LAA has, somehow, survived. The black cloud of eviction from the Thurmaston Lane premises in 1970 resulted in the move to the present site and allowed expansion of the Centre to what we see today. That cloud really did have a silver lining.

For all those who have acquired an animal, worked at, or supported, LAA in any way, the Centre holds a very special place in their hearts. It is that indefinable mix of friendship and family, combined with a real commitment to ensure the best possible standards of care for the dogs and cats that pass through the gates, that make it so special. True, the Centre has grown and expanded over the years, but it has still managed to retain its original values and atmosphere despite the introduction of health and safety regulation, and other animal welfare considerations, which must take precedence over free access to the animals in the care of LAA.

Anyone visiting the site in 2005 cannot fail to be impressed by the building revolution that has taken place, mainly over the last 7- 8 years. The kennel blocks and cattery are second to none, providing the best possible living conditions for the inmates, and the best possible working conditions for those caring for the animals. It is hard to remember the old wire runs yet they were still in evidence only as recently as six years ago. Fond as some may have been of the old portakabins that served as Reception and Office for so many years, there can be no doubt that the new Visitor and Education Centre opened early in 2005, is a tremendous facility that will only serve to enhance the work of LAA in the future, particularly as the education and community liaison role further develops. The site itself provides real opportunities for both conservation activity and education.

How many times is it said that it would be wonderful if animal rescue and rehoming centres, such as LAA, were no longer needed? No strays, no abandoned animals, no cruelty cases? Working to encourage responsible pet ownership is a key objective. The thriving junior arm of LAA – the Huncote Hound Club – has the potential to lay the foundations of a truly caring approach to animal welfare for its young members. Promoting neutering of cats and dogs is vital in reducing the number of unwanted cats and dogs, often abandoned to take their chance in life, and more often than not finding their way to LAA or one of the other animal rescue centres. LAA alone will not change a mindset, but working in partnership with Wood Green Animal Shelters and the other organisations that make up the Association of Cats and Dogs Homes, there is the opportunity to play a strategic and national role in animal welfare issues.

A real strength of Leicester Animal Aid, and one which must continue, is the service it provides to the community and particularly to those people who, through no fault of their own, such as old age, declining health or bereavement, find themselves unable to care for much loved pets and make the difficult decision to offer their pets up for rehoming. For those people there must always be somewhere to turn. Services include: the Pet SOS Service, under which pet owners can indicate that, in the event of their death, their pets should be taken in by LAA; the LAA Foster Scheme under which older animals are placed in homes so that they can live out their days in a loving environment, with vets bills being met in full or in part by LAA. Finally, the Petfinder Service, run in conjunction with Radio Leicester, plays a key role in helping to reunite lost pets with their owners.

Above: Huncote Hound Club August 2005

Right: Pet SOS Scheme leaflet

The tremendous hard work of all involved in seeing through the initial plans to the fabulous complex that now stands on the Huncote site cannot go to waste. We owe it to all who have supported LAA in the past, and those animals who may be in need of care, to ensure a secure future. This is the challenge facing the current management team. The challenges are very different from ten years ago, when replacing the old blocks and rebuilding the site was a clear and sometimes apparently unachievable dream. That dream was achieved. There is a new team in place. There is a clear strategy for the future. The same sense of drive and determination that has always prevailed will take LAA forward to the next ten years and beyond.

Below: Keely Short at the Family Fun Day August 2005

Leicester Animal Aid is hugely fortunate in the staff employed in the organisation. Keely Short, who took up the post of LAA General Manager at the end of June 2004, summed up the view of many. "I believe we're only as good as the team that cares for the animals and if that is true then we have one of the best rescue centres in the country. There really isn't such a thing as a '9 to 5' in animal rescue work! I'm proud of the level of commitment the staff show and their dedication to

Above: Team photo in front of new Visitor/Education Centre

giving the best they can to each and every animal that arrives at our door."

Securing the long-term financial future is the main challenge facing the Committee. Leicester Animal Aid receives no government funding and is competing for charitable donations at a time when charities are under increasing financial pressure. Legacy income, for many years, the lifeblood which enabled much of the building work to be undertaken, is at best unpredicatable and a sudden downturn in legacy income, such as experienced in mid 2005, can have an immediate and devastating impact.

Completion of the rebuilding programme means there will be no need for major capital expenditure for years to come, but buildings still need to be maintained, staff paid, and animals fed and provided with appropriate veterinary care. With running costs now in excess of £20,000 per month, the Committee faces a major challenge in ensuring a steady and reliable flow of income. The individual donor will always be important but securing more corporate funding, large grants, and legacies is critical for the future.

Below: Legacies and Bequests leaflet

In striving to secure a long-term future for Leicester Animal Aid, we should reflect on the words of the late Don Crowther, then Senior Trustee, and the person credited in the early 1990s with putting LAA on a more sound business footing. Don was quite clear. "LAA can go forwards or backwards. There is no standing still. But in fact there is no choice, we must go forwards, and we will. This means ensuring that the organisation is run as efficiently as possible, that all possible cost savings are made, but also that opportunities for fund raising and income generation are taken. In essence it means doing all we can to ensure that the Leicester Animal Aid vision is fulfilled."

Right: More team members

Don Crowther

REFLECTIONS

In concluding this celebration of the first fifty years of Leicester Animal Aid, it is interesting to speculate what founder, Dorothea Farndon, would make of all that has been achieved since she first started taking strays into her home.

"I always like to end the AGM by asking whether Mrs Farndon would have approved of what we're doing. I think she would. Well I hope she would. Yes, I'm sure she would – well, most of the time anyway!"

Janet Campion, LAA Chair
September 2005